The Battle Of The Falkland Islands Before And After

by
Henry Edmund Harvey Spencer-Cooper

The Battle Of
The Falkland Islands Before And After
by Henry Edmund Harvey Spencer-Cooper

Copyright © 2023

All Rights reserved.

No part of this publication may be reproduced, stored in a retrieval system, or transmitted in any form or by any means, electronic, mechanical, photocopying or Otherwise, without the written permission of the publisher.
The author/editor asserts the moral right to be identified as the author/editor of this work.

ISBN: 978-93-60469-64-1

Published by

DOUBLE 9 BOOKS
2/13-B, Ansari Road
Daryaganj, New Delhi – 110002
info@double9books.com
www.double9books.com
Tel. 011-40042856

This book is under public domain

ABOUT THE AUTHOR

Henry Edmund Harvey Spencer-Cooper's book, "The Battle of the Falkland Islands Before and After," stands as a masterpiece, showcasing his brilliance as a creator deeply engaged in historical analysis. With meticulous attempt, Spencer-Cooper crafts a narrative that now not only dissects navy activities but additionally builds a profound connection among the reader and the intricacies of history. His writing serves as a bridge, facilitating a connection amongst humans and fostering a higher know-how of the past. Spencer-Cooper's creativity and passion infuse life into his narratives, introducing readers to various geographical regions of history and evoking a variety of emotions. In his works, you can discover beauty and ease intertwined, creating a literary revel in that transcends complexity and allows a broad target market to revel in the richness of his top notch stories. Henry Edmund Harvey Spencer-Cooper's contributions to historical literature mirror no longer most effective his scholarly intensity but also his commitment to making history handy and engaging for every person. Through his stylish prose and compelling storytelling, he leaves an indelible mark, inviting readers to discover and respect the complexities of historic activities with both leisure and enlightenment.

CONTENTS

INTRODUCTION 7

Part I
EXPLOITS OFF SOUTH AMERICA 8

CHAPTER I
GERMAN MEN-OF-WAR IN FOREIGN SEAS 9

CHAPTER II
THE POLICY OF ADMIRAL COUNT VON SPEE 15

CHAPTER III
BRITISH MEN-OF-WAR OFF SOUTH AMERICA 19

CHAPTER IV
LIFE AT SEA IN 1914 25

CHAPTER V
THE SINKING OF THE "CAP TRAFALGAR" 29

CHAPTER VI
THE ACTION OFF CORONEL 35

CHAPTER VII
CONCENTRATION 45

CHAPTER VIII
POSSIBILITIES AND PROBABILITIES 49

Part II
THE BATTLE OF THE FALKLANDS 55

CHAPTER IX
AWAY SOUTH 57

CHAPTER X
ENEMY IN SIGHT 62

CHAPTER XI
THE BATTLE-CRUISER ACTION 68

CHAPTER XII
THE END OF THE "LEIPZIG" 76

CHAPTER XIII
THE SINKING OF THE "NÜRNBERG" 84

CHAPTER XIV
AFTERMATH 90

CHAPTER XV
THE PSYCHOLOGY OF THE SAILOR IN ACTION 94

CHAPTER XVI
VON SPEE'S AIMS AND HOPES 100

CHAPTER XVII
THE PARTING OF THE WAYS 105

CHAPTER XVIII
THE LAST OF THE "DRESDEN" 108

Part III

OFFICIAL DISPATCHES

I   DISPATCH OF THE ACTION OF H.M.S. "CARMANIA" 111

II DISPATCH OF THE ACTION FOUGHT OFF CORONEL 114

III OFFICIAL DISPATCH OF VICE-ADMIRAL COUNT VON SPEE 116

IV DISPATCH OF THE BATTLE OF THE FALKLAND ISLANDS 119

BATTLE OF FALKLAND ISLANDS, ... 127

THE "DRESDEN": ACTION WITH "KENT" AND "GLASGOW" 133

Appendix 134

INDEX 155

FOOTNOTES: 166

INTRODUCTION

This plain, unvarnished account, so far as is known, is the first attempt that has been made to link with the description of the Falkland Islands battle, fought on December 8th, 1914, the events leading up to that engagement.

In order to preserve accuracy as far as possible, each phase presented has been read and approved by officers who participated. The personal views expressed on debatable subjects, such as strategy, are sure to give rise to criticism, but it must be remembered that at the time of writing the exact positions of the ships engaged in overseas operations were not fully known, even in the Service.

The subject falls naturally into three divisions:

Part I. deals briefly with the movements of British and German warships, and includes the duel fought by the *Carmania*, and the action that took place off Coronel.

Part II. describes the Falkland Islands battle itself, and the subsequent fate of the German cruiser *Dresden*.

Part III. contains the official dispatches bearing on these exploits.

The words of Alfred Noyes have been referred to frequently, because they are in so many respects pro[xii]phetic, and also because of their influence in showing that the spirit of Drake still inspires the British Navy of to-day.

The author takes this opportunity of expressing his warmest thanks to those who have helped him in collecting information and in the compilation of this book.

Part I
EXPLOITS OFF SOUTH AMERICA

"Meekly content and tamely stay-at-home
The sea-birds seemed that piped across the waves;
And Drake, bemused, leaned smiling to his friend
Doughty and said, 'Is it not strange to know
When we return, yon speckled herring-gulls
Will still be wheeling, dipping, flashing there?
We shall not find a fairer land afar
Than those thyme-scented hills we leave behind!
Soon the young lambs will bleat across the combes,
And breezes will bring puffs of hawthorn scent
Down Devon lanes; over the purple moors
Lav'rocks will carol; and on the village greens
Around the maypole, while the moon hangs low,
The boys and girls of England merrily swing
In country footing through the flowery dance.'"

—Alfred Noyes (*Drake*).

CHAPTER I
GERMAN MEN-OF-WAR IN FOREIGN SEAS

"I, my Lords, have in different countries seen much of the miseries of war. I am, therefore, in my inmost soul, a man of peace. Yet I would not, for the sake of any peace, however fortunate, consent to sacrifice one jot of England's honour." —(*Speech by Lord Nelson in the House of Lords, November 16th, 1802.*)

We are now approaching the end of the third year of this great war,[1] and most Englishmen, having had some of the experience that war inevitably brings with it, will agree that the words which Nelson spoke are as true to-day as when they were uttered just over a century ago. Furthermore, as time and the war go on, the spirit of the whole British nation—be it man or woman—is put to an ever-increasing test of endurance, which is sustained and upheld by those two simple words, "England's Honour." An old platitude, "Might is Right," is constantly being quoted; but the nation that reverses the order is bound to outlast the other and win through to the desired goal. The justness of the cause, then, is the secret of our strength, which will not only endure but bring success to our arms in the end.

When Great Britain plunged into this Armageddon on August 4th, 1914, the only German squadron not in European waters was stationed in the Western Pacific, with its main base at Tsingtau. In addition there were a few German light cruisers isolated in various parts of the world, many of them being in proximity to British squadrons, which would point to the fact that Germany never really calculated on Great Britain throwing in her lot on the opposite side.

The recent troubles in Mexico accounted for the presence of both British and German cruisers in those waters, where they had been operating in conjunction with one another in the most complete harmony. As an instance, it might be mentioned that on August 2nd, 1914, one of our sloops was actually about to land a guard for one of our Consulates at a Mexican port in the boats belonging to a German light cruiser!

A short description of some of the movements of the German ships during the first few months of war will suffice to show that their primary object was to damage our overseas trade as much as possible. Further, since it is the fashion nowadays to overrate Germany's powers of organisation and skill, it will be interesting to observe that in spite of the vulnerability of our worldwide trade comparatively little was achieved.

The German squadron in China was under the command of Vice-Admiral Count von Spee. The outbreak of war found him on a cruise in the Pacific, which ultimately extended far beyond his expectations. The two armoured cruisers *Scharnhorst*—in which Admiral von Spee flew his flag—and *Gneisenau* left Nagasaki on June 28th, 1914. Their movements southward are of no particular interest until their arrival on July 7th at the Truk or Rug Islands, in the Caroline group, which then belonged to Germany. After a few days they leisurely continued their cruise amongst the islands of Polynesia. About the middle of the month the light cruiser *Nürnberg* was hastily recalled from San Francisco, and sailed on July 21st, joining von Spee's squadron at Ponape (also one of the Caroline Islands), where the three ships mobilised for war. On August 6th they sailed for an unknown destination, taking with them an auxiliary cruiser called the *Titania*.

THE WAR ZONE IN WESTERN SEAS

Apparently they were somewhat short of provisions, particularly of fresh meat and potatoes, for it was said in an intercepted letter that their diet consisted mainly of "spun yarn" (preserved meat).

On August 22nd the *Nürnberg* was sent to Honolulu to get papers and to send telegrams, rejoining the squadron shortly afterwards. A day or two later she was again detached, this time to Fanning Island, where she destroyed the British cable station, cut the cable, rejoining the squadron about September 7th, apparently at Christmas Island. Hearing that hostile forces were at Apia (Samoan Islands), von Spee sailed southward only to find, on his arrival, that it was empty of shipping.

The squadron now proceeded eastward to the French Society Islands to see what stores were to be found there. Completing supplies of coal at Bora Bora Island, it suddenly appeared off Papeete, the capital of Tahiti, on September 22nd. A French gunboat lying in the harbour was sunk by shellfire, the town and forts were subjected to a heavy bombardment, whilst the coal stores were set on fire. Calling in later at the Marquesas Islands, the German Admiral shaped his course eastward toward Easter Island, which was reached on October 12th.

The light cruiser *Leipzig* sailed from Mazatlan, an important town on the west coast of Mexico, on August 2nd. Ten days later she was reported off the entrance to Juan de Fuca Straits, between Vancouver and the mainland, but never ventured inside to attack the naval dockyard of Esquimalt. When war broke out the Canadian Government with great promptitude purchased two submarines from an American firm at Seattle; this was probably known to the Germans, and might account for their unwillingness to risk an attack on a port that was otherwise practically defenceless.

The Canadian light cruiser *Rainbow*, together with the British sloop *Algerine*, did excellent work on this coast. The former, in particular, showed much zeal in shadowing the *Leipzig*, though they never actually met.

The *Leipzig* achieved absolutely nothing worthy of note, although she remained on the west coast of America for a long time. It was not till the middle of October that she joined Admiral von Spee's squadron at Easter Island, without having caused any damage to the British Mercantile Marine.

The light cruiser *Dresden* was at St. Thomas, one of the larger of the Virgin Islands group, West Indies. She sailed on August 1st and proceeded straight to Cape Horn, only staying her career to coal at various places *en route* where she was unlikely to be reported. Crossing and re-crossing the trade route, she arrived on September 5th at Orange Bay, which is a large uninhabited natural harbour a few miles to the north-west of Cape Horn.

Here she was met by a collier, and stayed eleven days making adjustments to her engines. She evidently considered that she was now free from danger—we had no cruisers here at this period—for she continued her course into the Pacific, easing down to a speed of 8½ knots, and keeping more in the track of shipping. She met the German gunboat *Eber* on September 19th, to the northward of Magellan, and continued her way, apparently on the look out for allied commerce, but only succeeded in sinking two steamers before joining the flag of Admiral von Spee at Easter Island on October 12th. Altogether she sank three steamers and four sailing vessels, representing a total value of just over £250,000.

The light cruiser *Karlsruhe*, the fastest and most modern of the German ships on foreign service, was in the Gulf of Mexico at the commencement of the war. On her way to her sphere of operations in the neighbourhood of Pernambuco she was sighted on August 6th, whilst coaling at sea from the armed liner *Kronprinz Wilhelm*, by the British cruiser *Suffolk*. Admiral Cradock, who was then flying his flag in the *Suffolk*, immediately gave chase to the *Karlsruhe*, the *Kronprinz Wilhelm* bolting in the opposite direction. During the forenoon Admiral Cradock called up by wireless the light cruiser *Bristol*, which was in the vicinity, and, giving her the position of the *Karlsruhe*, ordered her to intercept the enemy. The *Karlsruhe* was kept in sight by the *Suffolk* for several hours, but was never within gun-range, and finally escaped from her by superior speed. It was a beautiful moonlight evening when the *Bristol* sighted her quarry at 8 P.M., and a quarter of an hour later opened fire, which was returned a few moments later by the *Karlsruhe*, but it was too dark for either ship to see the results of their shooting. All the enemy's shots fell short, so that the *Bristol* incurred no damage. Both ships went on firing for fifty-five minutes, by which time the German had drawn out of range. Admiral Cradock signalled during the action, "Stick to it—I am coming"; all this time the *Suffolk* was doing her best to catch up, but never succeeded in reaching the scene of the first naval action in the world-war. The German disappeared in the darkness, and was never seen again by our warships.

In her subsequent raids on British commerce along the South Atlantic trade routes the *Karlsruhe* was, on the whole, successful, until she met a sudden and inglorious end off Central America. Her fate was for a long time shrouded in mystery, the first clue being some of her wreckage, which was found washed up on the shores of the island of St. Vincent in the West Indies. Some of her survivors eventually found their way back to the Fatherland and reported that she had foundered with 260 officers and men—due to an internal explosion on November 4th, 1914, in latitude 10° 07′ N., longitude 55° 25′ W. (*See* Map)

In all she sank seventeen ships, representing a value of £1,622,000.

There remain three German armed merchant cruisers that claim our attention on account of their operations off South America. The *Cap Trafalgar* only existed for a month before being sunk by the armed Cunard liner *Carmania*. A description of the fight is given in a subsequent chapter.

The *Prinz Eitel Friedrich* was more directly under the orders of Admiral von Spee, and acted in conjunction with his squadron in the Pacific until the battle of the Falkland Islands, when she operated on her own account against our trade with South America. She achieved some measure of success during the few months that she was free, and captured ten ships altogether, several of which, however, were sailing vessels. Early in March she arrived at Newport News in the United States with a number of prisoners on board, who had been taken from these prizes. She was badly in need of refit; her engines required repairs, and the Germans fondly imagined that they might escape internment. On hearing that one of her victims was an American vessel, public indignation was hotly aroused and but little sympathy was shown for her wants. Her days of marauding were brought to an abrupt termination, for the Americans resolutely interned her.

Lastly, there was the *Kronprinz Wilhelm*, which, as we have seen, was in company with the *Karlsruhe* when the latter was sighted and chased by the *Suffolk* only two days after war was declared. She was commanded by one of the officers of the *Karlsruhe*, and worked under her orders in the Atlantic. In fact, the German cruiser transferred two of her Q.F. guns to the armed merchantman, and they were mounted on her forecastle. She was skilful in avoiding our cruisers and literally fed upon her captures, being fortunate in obtaining coal with fair frequency. In the course of eight months the *Kronprinz Wilhelm* captured and destroyed fifteen British or French ships, four of which were sailing vessels. It will be realised how small was the toll of our ships sailing these seas, especially when it is recollected that the main object of the Germans at this time was to make war on our maritime trade. Finally, sickness broke out on board and there were several cases of beriberi; moreover, the ship leaked and was in want of repairs, so on April 11th she also steamed into Newport News and was interned.

That the Germans did not approach the results they hoped for in attacking our commerce was in a large measure due to the unceasing activity of our cruisers, who forced the German ships to be continually on the move to fresh hunting grounds. Thus, although many of them escaped capture or destruction for some time, they were perpetually being disturbed and hindered in their work of depredation.

The exploits of the light cruisers *Emden* and *Königsberg* are outside the scope of this book, but the following brief summary may be of interest.

Sailing from Tsingtau on August 5th, with four colliers, the *Emden* apparently proceeded to cruise in the neighbourhood of Vladivostock, where she captured a Russian auxiliary cruiser and one or two merchant ships, before going south to make history in the Bay of Bengal. She was eventually brought to book off the Cocos Islands on November 9th, 1914, by the Australian light cruiser *Sydney*, in a very gallant action which lasted over an hour and a half, when she ran herself ashore in a sinking condition on North Keeling Island. She sank seventeen ships all told, representing a total value of £2,211,000.

The *Königsberg*, at the commencement of hostilities, was lying at Dar-es-Salaam, the capital of what was formerly German East Africa. She sank the *Pegasus*, a light cruiser only two-thirds of her size and of much inferior armament, at Zanzibar on September 20th, but only succeeded in sinking one or two steamers afterwards. She was eventually discovered hiding in the Rufiji Delta in German East Africa, towards the end of October, 1914, where she was kept blocked up by our ships for nearly nine months. Finally, on July 11th, 1915, she was destroyed by gunfire by the monitors *Severn* and *Mersey*, who went up the river—the banks on both sides being entrenched—and reduced her to a hopeless wreck where she lay, some fourteen miles from the sea.

CHAPTER II
THE POLICY OF ADMIRAL COUNT VON SPEE

It is clearly impossible to state with any exactitude the motives which governed von Spee's policy; but, in briefly reviewing the results, a shrewd idea of the reasons which led him to certain conclusions may be formed. Also, it will assist the reader to a conclusion on the merits and demerits of the strategy adopted, and will help him to follow more easily the reasons for some of the movements of our own ships described in the next chapter.

That Admiral von Spee did not return to Tsingtau at the outbreak of hostilities appears significant, since he was by no means inferior to our squadron, and wished to mobilise his ships. He, however, sent the *Emden* there with dispatches and instructions to the colliers about meeting him after she had escorted them to sea. Japan, it will be remembered, did not declare war till August 23rd, 1914, and therefore could scarcely have come into his earlier calculations. His action in continuing his cruise in the Southern Pacific, where he was handy and ready to strike at the French colonies[2] at the psychological moment of the outbreak of hostilities, gives the impression that he did not consider England's intervention probable.

Previous to the war, the *Leipzig* and *Nürnberg* had been detached to the West Coast of America, and it appears likely that von Spee was influenced in his decision to remain at large in the Pacific by this fact, as, before this dispersal of his squadron, he would have been distinctly superior to the British Fleet in the China Station at that time. Great care was taken by him to keep all his movements secret, and he appears to have avoided making many wireless signals.

The decision of the British Government to proceed with operations against the German colonies in the Southern Pacific must have had a determining effect on German policy; this decision was made at the very outset and allowed the enemy no time to make preparations to counter it. The value of the patriotism and loyal co-operation of the Dominions in building up their own Navy in peace time was now clearly demonstrated, Australia being the first of our Dominions to embark on this policy.

The German China squadron was inferior in strength to our ships in Australian waters, and could not afford to risk encountering the powerful battle-cruiser *Australia* with her eight 12-inch guns; consequently, von Spee was compelled to abandon the many colonies in Polynesia to their fate. Finally, the advent of Japan into the conflict left him little choice but to make his way to the eastward, since not to do so was to court almost certain destruction, while to move west and conceal his whereabouts was an impossibility. That von Spee felt his position to be precarious, and had difficulty in making up his mind what to do, is shown by the slow and indecisive movement of his squadron at first.

The movements of the German light cruisers lead to the conclusion that they must have received orders to scatter so as to destroy our trade in various spheres. The *Leipzig* apparently patrolled the western side of North America, whilst the *Karlsruhe* took the South Atlantic, and so on.

Why the *Dresden* should have steamed over 6,000 miles to the Pacific instead of assisting the *Karlsruhe* is hard to explain, unless she had direct orders from the German Admiralty. She could always have joined von Spee later.

With the exception of the *Emden*, who operated with success in the Bay of Bengal, and the *Karlsruhe*, whose area of operations was along the junction of the South Atlantic and the West Indian trade routes, none of them succeeded in accomplishing a fraction of the damage that might reasonably have been expected at a time when our merchantmen were not organised for war and business was "as usual." It cannot be denied that the *Emden's* raids wholly disorganised the trade along the east coast of India. The local moneylenders—who are the bankers to the peasants—abandoned the coast completely, trade nearly came to a standstill, and the damage done took months to recover. In this case the effects could by no means be measured by an armchair calculation of the tonnage sunk by the *Emden* in pounds, shillings and pence.

The main anxiety of the German Admiral lay in the continuance of his supplies, which could only be assured by careful organisation. This was rendered comparatively easy in South America, where every port teemed with Germans; the wheels of communication, through the agency of shore wireless stations, were well oiled by German money, and there were numerous German merchantmen, fitted with wireless, ready to hand to be used as supply ships or colliers.

It was thus of paramount importance that the German Squadron should be rounded up and annihilated before it could become a serious menace to our trade and that of our Allies. The other remaining light cruisers of the enemy, who were operating singly, could be dealt with more easily, since our ships could afford to separate in order to search for them, thus rendering it only a matter of time before they were destroyed.

What was the object, then, of the German Admiral? This was the all-important question that occupied the thoughts of all our naval officers in foreign parts. On the assumption that he would come eastwards, there appeared to be few choices open to him beyond the following:

(1) To bombard the seaports of our colonies on the west coast of Africa and to attack weakly defended but by no means valueless naval stations (such as St. Helena), at the same time operating against British and French expeditions going by sea against German colonies.

(2) To go to South Africa, destroy the weak British squadron at the Cape, and hang up Botha's expedition by supporting a rising against us in the South African Dominions.

(3) To endeavour to make his way home to Germany.

(4) To operate in the North Atlantic.

(5) To harass our trade with South America.

Both the first and second appeared quite feasible, but they had the twofold disadvantage of involving actions nearer England and of very possibly restricting the enemy a good deal in his movements; there are few harbours on this coast, and his every movement would become known in a region where we held the monopoly in methods of communication. Consequently, any success here was bound to be more or less short-lived. On the other hand, matters were undoubtedly very critical in these parts. De la Rey, when he was shot, was actually on his way to raise the Vierkleur at Potchefstroom, and any striking naval success which it would have taken us three weeks to deal with at the very least, might have just set the balance against us at this time in the minds of the waverers. Moreover, it would not have been difficult to ensure supplies from the German colonies.

The third may be dismissed as being extremely improbable at the outset, for it is difficult to run a blockade with a number of ships, and, for the enemy, it would too much have resembled thrusting his head into the lion's jaws. Besides, he could be of far greater service to his country in roaming the seas and in continuing to be a thorn in our side as long as possible.

The fourth will scarcely bear examination; cut off from all bases, he could hardly hope to escape early destruction.

The fifth seemed by far the most favourable to his hopes, as being likely to yield a richer harvest, and, if successful, might paralyse our enormous trade with South America, upon which we were so dependent.

German influence was predominant as well as unscrupulous along the Brazilian coasts, which would render it easy to maintain supplies. To evoke sympathy amongst the smaller Republics would also come within his horizon. Finally, he could have had little idea of our strength in South Africa; whereas information gleaned from Valparaiso (which von Spee evidently considered reliable) as to the precise extent of our limited naval resources then on the east coast of South America, must have proved a deciding factor in determining his strategy.

Whichever course were adopted, it was practically certain that the German Admiral would move eastwards, either through the Straits of Magellan or, more probably, round the Horn to avoid having his whereabouts reported. That this occurred to the minds of our naval authorities before the action off Coronel took place is practically certain, but it is to be regretted that reinforcements to Admiral Cradock's squadron operating in South American waters were not sent there in time to prevent that disaster.

This, then, in brief, was the problem that presented itself to our commanders after the battle of Coronel took place, and no doubt influenced them in the choice of the Falkland Islands as a base, its geographical position making it almost ideal in the event of any move in that direction on the part of the Germans.

CHAPTER III
BRITISH MEN-OF-WAR OFF SOUTH AMERICA

"If England hold
The sea, she holds the hundred thousand gates
That open to futurity. She holds
The highways of all ages. Argosies
Of unknown glory set their sails this day
For England out of ports beyond the stars.
Ay, on the sacred seas we ne'er shall know
They hoist their sails this day by peaceful quays,
Great gleaming wharves i' the perfect City of God,
If she but claims her heritage."

—Alfred Noyes (*Drake*).

Before attempting to give a description of the battle of the Falkland Islands, it is necessary to review very briefly the movements and dispositions of our ships, as well as the events preceding the battle, which include both the duel between the armed merchant cruiser *Carmania* and *Cap Trafalgar* and the action fought off Coronel on the coast of Chile by Admiral Cradock.

Our naval forces were scattered in comparatively small units all over the world when war broke out. Ships in various squadrons were separated from one another by great distances, and, with the exception of our Mediterranean Fleet, we possessed no squadron in any part of the globe equal in strength to that of von Spee.

Attention is directed to the positions of Easter Island, where the Germans had last been reported, Valparaiso, Coronel, Magellan Straits, Staten Island, the Falkland Islands, Buenos Ayres, Montevideo, Rio de Janeiro, Pernambuco, and the Island of Trinidad off the east coast of South America, since they occur continually in the course of this narrative.[3]

In the early part of 1914 Rear-Admiral Sir Christopher Cradock, K.C.V.O., C.B., flying his flag in the *Suffolk*, was in command of the fourth cruiser squadron, which was then doing some very useful work in the

Gulf of Mexico. On August 2nd he was at Kingston, Jamaica, and received information that the *Good Hope* was on her way out to become his flagship, so he sailed northwards to meet her. On the way he sighted and gave chase to the *Karlsruhe* on August 6th, as has been related. The *Suffolk* and the *Good Hope* met at sea ten days later, and the Admiral went on board the latter immediately and hoisted his flag.

Turning south, he went to Bermuda, called in at St. Lucia on August 23rd, and thence proceeded along the north coast of South America on his way to take up the command of a newly forming squadron of British ships patrolling the trade routes and protecting the merchant shipping in South American waters. At St. Lucia Admiral Cradock would probably have learned of the sailing of von Spee's squadron from Ponape on August 6th, and this accounts for his haste in making south in order to meet and form his ships together.

The squadron was gradually augmented as time went on, and in the months of September and October, 1914, consisted of the flagship *Good Hope* (Captain Philip Francklin), *Canopus* (Captain Heathcoat Grant), *Monmouth* (Captain Frank Brandt), *Cornwall* (Captain W. M. Ellerton), *Glasgow* (Captain John Luce), *Bristol* (Captain B. H. Fanshawe), and the armed merchant cruisers *Otranto* (Captain H. McI. Edwards), *Macedonia* (Captain B. S. Evans), and *Orama* (Captain J. R. Segrave).

No news was obtainable as to the whereabouts of the German squadron stationed in the Pacific, which consisted of the *Scharnhorst, Gneisenau, Emden, Nürnberg,* and *Leipzig,* except that it was known that the two latter had been operating on the east side of the Pacific, and that the *Emden* was in the Bay of Bengal. The vaguest rumours, all contradicting one another, were continually being circulated, in which it is more than likely that German agents had a large share.

Admiral Cradock proceeded south in the middle of September to watch the Straits of Magellan, and to patrol between there and the River Plate, as he doubtless hoped to prevent the *Karlsruhe* and *Dresden*—which, when last heard of, were in South American waters—from attempting to effect a junction with their main squadron. With him were the *Monmouth, Glasgow,* and the armed Orient liner *Otranto,* in addition to his own ship the *Good Hope,* which, together with his colliers, had their first base in the Falkland Islands.

On hearing of the appearance of the Germans off Papeete and of the bombardment of the French colony there on September 22nd, it was apparently considered expedient to proceed to the west coast of South America in order to intercept the enemy. Accordingly, early in October the *Monmouth, Glasgow,* and *Otranto* went round to the Pacific, diligently searching out the many inlets and harbours *en route,* and arrived at Valparaiso on October 15th, but only stayed a part of one day in order to get stores and provisions. They then went back southwards to meet the *Good Hope* and *Canopus,* vainly hoping to fall in with the *Leipzig* or *Dresden* on the way. The *Good Hope* reached the Chilean coast on October 29th, and all ships filled up with coal; the *Canopus* was due very shortly, and actually sighted our ships steaming off as she arrived.

In order to carry out a thorough and effective examination of the innumerable inlets that abound amongst the channels of Tierra del Fuego, in addition to the bays and harbours on both coasts of South America, it became necessary to divide up this squadron into separate units. To expedite matters, colliers were sent to meet our ships, so that valuable time should not be lost in returning to the base at the Falkland Islands. The first fine day was seized to fill up with coal, care always being taken to keep outside the three-mile territorial limit.

It must have been a trying and anxious time for both officers and men, while pursuing their quest, never knowing what force might suddenly be disclosed in opening out one of these harbours. From the weather usually experienced in these parts some idea may be formed of the discomforts. An officer in the *Glasgow,* writing of this period, says: "It blew, snowed, rained, hailed, and sleeted as hard as it is possible to do these things. I thought the ship would dive under altogether at times. It was a short sea, and very high, and doesn't suit this ship a bit. The *Monmouth* was rather worse, if anything, though not quite so wet. We were rolling 35 degrees, and quite useless for fighting purposes. The ship was practically a submarine."

Imagine, too, the position of the *Otranto,* searching these waters by herself, without the least hope of being able to fight on level terms with one of the enemy's light-cruisers. The words of one of her officers sum up the situation: "We finally got past caring what might happen," he said; "what with the strain, the weather, and the extreme cold, we longed to find something and to have it out, one way or the other."

When the depredations of the *Karlsruhe* became more numerous, the Admiralty dispatched ships—as could best be spared from watching other trade routes—to reinforce Admiral Cradock's command. Thus, what may be termed a second squadron was formed, consisting of the *Canopus, Cornwall, Bristol,* the armed P. & O. liner *Macedonia,* and the armed Orient liner *Orama.* This latter squadron carried out a fruitless search during September and October for the ever elusive *Karlsruhe,* but, so far as is known, did not succeed in getting near her, for she was never actually sighted. In the absence of orders from Admiral Cradock, the duties of Senior Naval Officer of this northern squadron frequently involved the consideration of matters of no little consequence. These duties primarily devolved upon the shoulders of Captain Fanshawe of the *Bristol*, who was succeeded on the arrival of the *Canopus* by Captain Heathcoat Grant. As the poor state of the engines of the *Canopus* did not enable her to steam at any speed, she remained at the base and directed operations, forming a valuable link with her wireless. Orders, however, were received from Admiral Cradock which necessitated her sailing on October 10th in order to join his southern squadron, so that Captain Fanshawe was again left in command.

On October 24th the *Carnarvon* (Captain H. L. d'E. Skipwith) arrived, flying the flag of Rear-Admiral A. P. Stoddart, who, though acting under the orders of Admiral Cradock, now took charge of the sweeping operations necessitated by our quest. Admiral Stoddart had previously been in command of the ships operating along our trade routes near the Cape Verde Islands, where the *Carnarvon* had not long before made a valuable capture, the German storeship *Professor Woermann*, filled with coal and ammunition.

The comparatively large number of men-of-war mentioned is accounted for by the fact that at this time the *Karlsruhe* began to make her presence felt by sinking more merchant ships, which caused no little apprehension amongst the mercantile communities in all the ports on the north and east coasts of South America, Brazilian firms at this period refusing to ship their goods in British bottoms, although some British vessels were lying in harbour awaiting cargoes. The German ship's activities were mainly confined to the neighbourhood of St. Paul's Rocks, Pernambuco, and the Equator.

It is not easy to put clearly the disposition of the ships acting under Admiral Cradock at this time, nor to give an adequate idea of the many disadvantages with which he had to contend. The difficulties of communication on the east coast of South America between his two squadrons were very great, on account of the long distances between them (often some thousands of miles and always greater than the range of our wireless). The only method found feasible was to send messages in code by means of passing British merchantmen—usually the Royal Mail liners. The inevitable result of this was that it was frequently impossible for Admiral Cradock to keep in touch with his northern squadron, and important matters of policy had thus to be decided on the spot, the Admiral being informed later.

On the rare occasions that our ships visited Brazilian ports, which were crowded with German shipping, the crews of these ships, having nothing better to do, would come and pull round our cruisers—in all probability cursing us heartily the while—much to the interest and amusement of our men. These visits could only take place at the most once every three months, when the opportunity of getting a good square meal at a civilised restaurant was hailed with delight by those officers who were off duty.

Our coaling base in these waters was admirably selected. There was sufficient anchorage for a large number of ships four or five miles from any land, but protected from anything but a heavy swell or sea by surrounding ledges of coral awash at low water. Sometimes colliers got slightly damaged by bumping against our ships when there was a swell, but in other respects it suited its purpose excellently. The Brazilians sent a destroyer to investigate once or twice, but could find nothing to arouse their susceptibilities, for our ships were always well outside the three-mile limit. Our sole amusement was fishing, frequently for sharks.

Towards the latter part of August, the armed merchant cruiser *Carmania* (Captain Noel Grant) was sent out to join Admiral Cradock's squadron with coal, provisions, and a large quantity of frozen meat, which was sadly needed. She was ordered by him to assist the *Cornwall* in watching Pernambuco on September 11th, as it was thought that the German storeship *Patagonia* was going to put to sea on September 11th to join the *Karlsruhe*. On her way south she got orders to search Trinidad Island in the South Atlantic to find out whether the Germans were making use of it as a coaling base, and there fell in with the German armed liner *Cap Trafalgar*, which she sank in a very gallant action that is described in a subsequent chapter.

The armed merchant cruiser *Edinburgh Castle* (Captain W. R. Napier) was sent out from England with drafts of seamen and boys, as well as provisions and stores for our men-of-war in these waters. On her arrival at the base on October 12th, she was detained on service to assist in the sweep that had been organised to search for the *Karlsruhe*. Some of us have pleasant recollections of excellent games of deck hockey played on the spacious promenade deck during her all too short stay with us.

The *Defence* (Captain E. La T. Leatham) touched at the base to coal on October 27th, being on her way south to join Admiral Cradock's southern command. She had to coal in bad weather, and perforated the collier's side in doing so, but succeeded in completing with coal in the minimum possible time under difficult conditions. Without loss of time she proceeded to Montevideo, but never got any farther, as it was there that the news of the Coronel disaster first reached her. Admiral Cradock hoped to find von Spee before the German light-cruisers *Dresden* and *Leipzig* joined the main squadron; but he also was most anxious to wait for the *Defence*. She would have made a very powerful addition to his squadron, and it seems a thousand pities that it was not possible to effect this junction before he quitted the eastern shores of South America for the Pacific.

The *Defence* was very unlucky, and had a great deal of hard work without any kudos; not till Admiral Sturdee's arrival did she leave to join the *Minotaur* on the Cape of Good Hope station, and the very day she arrived there got the news of the Falkland Islands battle! Having covered 23,000 miles in two and a half months, the disappointment at having missed that fight was, of course, intense. It is sad to think that few of her gallant crew are alive to-day, as she was afterwards sunk in the battle of Jutland.

The *Invincible*, flagship of Vice-Admiral F. C. Doveton Sturdee (Captain P. H. Beamish), the *Inflexible* (Captain R. F. Phillimore, C.B., M.V.O.), and the *Kent* (Captain J. D. Allen) enter the scene of operations later.

CHAPTER IV
LIFE AT SEA IN 1914

"A seaman, smiling, swaggered out of the inn,
Swinging in one brown hand a gleaming cage
Wherein a big green parrot chattered and clung
Fluttering against the wires."

—Alfred Noyes (*Drake*).

A short digression may perhaps be permitted, if it can portray the long days, when for months at a time little occurs to break the monotony of sea life. The reader may also experience the charitable feeling that, at the expense of his patience, the sailor is indulging in the "grouse" that proverbially is supposed to be so dear to him.

Of necessity, work on board ship in wartime must be largely a matter of routine; and, though varied as much as possible, it tends to relapse into "the trivial round, the common task." All day and all night men man the guns ready to blaze off at any instant, extra look-outs are posted, and there are officers and men in the control positions. The ship's company is usually organised into three watches at night, which take turns in relieving one another every four hours.

After sunrise the increased visibility gives ample warning of any possible attack. The messdecks, guns, and ship generally are cleaned before breakfast, while the forenoon soon passes in perfecting the guns' crews and controls, and in physical drill. After dinner at noon and a smoke, everyone follows the old custom of the sea, and has a caulk (a sleep)—a custom originated in the days of sailing ships who were at sea for long periods at a time, and watch and watch (i.e. one watch on and one off) had to be maintained both day and night. The men lie about the decks, too tired to feel the want of either mattresses or pillows. The first dog watch (4–6 P.M.) is usually given up to recreation until sunset, when it is time to go to night defence stations. Day in and day out, this programme is seldom varied except to stop and examine a merchant ship now and again.

Every ship met with on the high seas is boarded for the examination of its passengers and cargo, an undertaking often attended by some difficulty on a dark night. On approaching, it is customary to signal the ship to stop; if this is not obeyed at once, a blank round is fired as a warning; should this be disregarded a shotted round is fired across her bows, but it is seldom necessary to resort to this measure. At night these excursions have a strange, unreal effect, and our boarding officer used to say that when climbing up a merchantman's side in rough weather he felt like some character in a pirate story. Getting out of a boat, as it is tossing alongside, on to a rope ladder, is by no means an easy job, especially if the officer is inclined to be portly. The searchlight, too, turned full on to the ship, blinding the scared passengers who come tumbling up, frequently imagining they have been torpedoed, adds to the mysterious effect produced, whilst the sudden appearance of the boarding officer in his night kit suggests a visit from Father Neptune. But any idea of comedy is soon shattered by the grumpy voice of the captain who has been turned out from his beauty sleep, or by the vehement objections of a lady or her husband to their cabin being searched. As a matter of fact, we were always met with the most unfailing courtesy, and the boat's crew was often loaded with presents of cigarettes or even chocolates, besides parcels of newspapers hastily made up and thrown down at the last moment.

Off a neutral coast the food problem is an everlasting difficulty, and as soon as the canteen runs out and tinned stores cannot be replenished, the menu resolves itself into a more or less fixed item of salt beef ("salt horse") or salt pork with pea soup. The old saying, "Feed the brute, if a man is to be kept happy," has proved itself true, but is one which at sea is often extraordinarily hard to follow, especially when it is impossible to get such luxuries as eggs, potatoes, and fresh meat. If flour runs out, the ship's biscuit ("hard tack"), which often requires a heavy blow to break it, forms but a poor substitute for bread; although it is quite good eating, a little goes a long way. The joy with which the advent of an armed liner is heralded by the officers cannot well be exaggerated; the stewards from all ships lose no time in trying to get all they can, and the memory of the first excellent meal is not easily forgotten.

The ever-recurring delight of coaling ship is looked forward to directly anchorage is reached. Coal-dust then penetrates everywhere, even to the food, and after a couple of hours it seems impossible for the ship ever to be clean again. Nearly every officer and man on board, including the chaplain and paymasters, join in the work, which continues day and night, as a rule, until finished. If this takes more than twenty-four hours there is the awful trial of sleeping, clothes and all, covered in grime, for hammocks have to be foregone, else they would be quite unfit for further use. The men wear any clothes they like. In the tropics it is a warm job working in the holds, and clothes are somewhat scanty. A very popular article is a bashed-in bowler hat, frequently worn with white shorts, and a football jersey! There is, generally, a wag amongst the men who keeps them cheery and happy, even during a tropical rain storm. His powers of mimicking, often ranging from politicians to gunnery instructors, bring forth rounds of applause, and all the time he'll dig out like a Trojan.

The sailor is a cheery bird, and seldom lets an opportunity of amusement escape. On one occasion, when lying at anchor in the tropics, someone suggested fishing; after the first fish had been caught many rods and lines were soon going. A would-be wit enlivened matters by tying an empty soda-water bottle on to a rather excitable man's line while he was away, which met with great success on the owner crying out, "I've got a real big 'un here" as he carefully played it to the delight of everyone. Shark fishing was a favourite sport, and three were caught and landed in one afternoon; one of them had three small sharks inside it.

The band (very few ships had the good fortune to possess one) plays from 4.30 to 5.30 P.M., when Jack disports himself in Mazurkas and d'Alberts, and dances uncommonly well before a very critical audience. Some men are always busy at their sewing machines when off duty, making clothes for their messmates; this they call "jewing"; others are barbers, or bootmakers, and they make quite a good thing out of it. Now that masts and sails are things of the past, substitutes in the way of exercise are very necessary, particularly when living on salt food. Boxing is greatly encouraged, and if competitions are organised, men go into strict training and the greatest keenness prevails. A canvas salt-water bath is usually rigged, and is in constant demand with the younger men. The officers congregate in flannels on the quarter-deck playing quoits, deck tennis, or cricket; some go in for doing Swedish exercises, Müller, or club swinging, and, to finish up with, a party is formed to run round the decks.

The Admiralty are extraordinarily good about dispatching mails to our ships, but sudden and unexpected movements often make it impossible to receive them with any regularity. When war broke out everyone wondered how their folk at home would manage, whether money and food would be easily obtainable. In our own case we were moved from our original sphere of operations, and did not get our first mail till October 19th, over eleven weeks after leaving England, and many other ships may have fared even worse. Again, our Christmas mail of 1914 was not received till six months afterwards, having followed us to the Falkland Islands, then back home, out again round the Cape of Good Hope, finally arriving at the Dardanelles. On this occasion one of the men had a pound of mutton and a plum pudding sent him by his wife; it can easily be imagined with what delight he welcomed these delicacies, which had been through the tropics several times, as did those others whose parcels were anywhere near his in the mail bag. It may appear a paltry thing to those who get their daily post regularly, but the arrival of a mail at sea is a very real joy, even to those who get but few letters. The newspapers are eagerly devoured, and events, whose bare occurrence may have only become known through meagre wireless communiqués, are at length made comprehensible.

Darkening ship at sunset is uncomfortable, more particularly in the tropics, when the heat on the messdecks becomes unbearable from lack of air. However, this is now much improved by supplying wind-scoops for the scuttles, fitted with baffles to prevent the light from showing outboard. Everyone sleeps on deck who can, risking the pleasures of being trodden upon in the dark, or of being drenched by a sudden tropical shower, when the scrum of men hastily snatching up their hammocks and running for the hatches equals that of any crowd at a football match. On moonless nights little diversions are constantly occurring. A certain officer, perfectly sober, on one occasion walked over the edge of the boat-deck into space, and then was surprised to find that he was hurt.

The hardships and anxieties of the life are probably overrated by people ashore. The very routine helps to make the sailor accustomed to the strange and unnatural conditions, nearly all of which have their humorous side. As is the way of the world, we on the coast of South America all envied those in the Grand Fleet at this time, in modern ships fitted with refrigerating rooms and plenty of good fresh food; and they, no doubt, willingly would have changed places with us, being sick to death of the uneventful life, cold, rough weather, and constant submarine strain from which we were fortunately immune. Events took such a shape a few months later that those of us who were fortunate enough to be in the battle of the Falkland Islands would not have been elsewhere for all the world.

CHAPTER V
THE SINKING OF THE "CAP TRAFALGAR"

"When, with a roar that seemed to buffet the heavens
And rip the heart of the sea out, one red flame
Blackened with fragments, the great galleon burst
Asunder! All the startled waves were strewn
With wreckage; and Drake laughed: 'My lads, we have diced
With death to-day, and won!'"

—Alfred Noyes (*Drake*).

It has already been mentioned that the *Carmania* was ordered to search the Brazilian island of Trinidad (not to be confused with the British Island of the same name), which lies in the South Atlantic about 600 miles to the eastward of South America, and in about the same latitude as Rio de Janeiro. It was uninhabited at this time, and seemed a likely place for the Germans to use as a temporary coaling base; they have never had any compunction about breaking the laws of neutrality if it suited their purpose.

The following narrative is taken from the official report, supplemented by an account written by the author two days after the action from a description given him by the officers of H.M.S. *Carmania*.

Land was sighted on the morning of September 14th, 1914. A moderate breeze was blowing from the north-east, but it was a lovely day, with a clear sky and the sun shining. Shortly after 11 A.M. the masts of a vessel were observed, and on approaching nearer the *Carmania* made out three steamers, apparently at anchor in a small bay that lies to the south-west of the island. One of these was a large liner, but the others were clearly colliers and had their derricks topped; they were probably working when they sighted us, and they immediately separated and made off in different directions before the whole of their hulls could be distinguished.

The large vessel was apparently a liner about equal in size,[4] having two funnels which were painted to resemble those of a Union Castle liner. After running away for a while, the larger steamer, which turned out to be the *Cap Trafalgar* (though this was not known for certain till weeks afterwards), altered course to starboard and headed more in our direction. She was then steering about south at what appeared to be full speed, while the *Carmania* was steaming 16 knots on a sou'-westerly course.

There could no longer be any doubt that she meant to fight, and the duel now ensued that has been so happily described by a gifted naval writer, the late Fred T. Jane, as "the Battle of the Haystacks." To my idea, it appears almost a replica of the frigate actions of bygone days, and will probably go down in history as a parallel to the engagement fought between the *Chesapeake* and *Shannon*. For gallantry, pluck and determination it certainly bears comparison with many of these actions of the past.

About noon she fired a single shot across the enemy's bows at a range of 8,500 yards, whereupon he immediately opened fire from his after-gun on the starboard side. This was quickly followed on both sides by salvoes (all guns firing nearly simultaneously as soon as their sights came on to the target), so matters at once became lively.

Curiously enough, the enemy's first few shots fell short, ricocheting over, and then, as the range decreased, they went clean over the hull, in consequence of which our rigging, masts, funnels, derricks, and ventilators all suffered, though the ship's side near the waterline—the principal anxiety—was so far intact. Some of the *Carmania's* first shots, which were fired at a range of 7,500 yards, were seen to take effect, and she continued to score hits afterwards with moderate frequency. The port battery was engaging his starboard guns at this period, so that he was on her port hand, and a reference to the plan will show that she was ahead on bearing. The range was rapidly decreasing since they were both on converging courses, but unfortunately the German ship had the speed of her, for the Cunarder could only do 16 knots, due largely to a lack of vacuum in the condensers. As far as could be judged the *Cap Trafalgar* was steaming between 17 and 18 knots. (*See* Diagram,)

At 4,500 yards, two of our broadsides were seen to hit all along the waterline. As the range decreased to 4,000 yards the shot from the enemy's pom-poms (machine guns), fired with great rapidity, began to fall like hail on and all round the ship; this induced Captain Grant to alter course away with promptitude, thus opening out the range and bringing the starboard battery into play. The port 4.7-inch guns—they were all over twenty years old—were by this time wellnigh red-hot. That the enemy did not apprehend this manœuvre was demonstrated by his erratic fire at this moment, when the Britisher was enabled to bring five guns into action to his four through being able to use both the stern guns. It was now that the German suffered most heavily, the havoc wrought in such a short time being very noticeable. He then turned away, which brought the two ships nearly stern on to one another; two of his steam pipes were cut by shell, the steam rising into the sky, he was well on fire forward, and had a list to starboard.

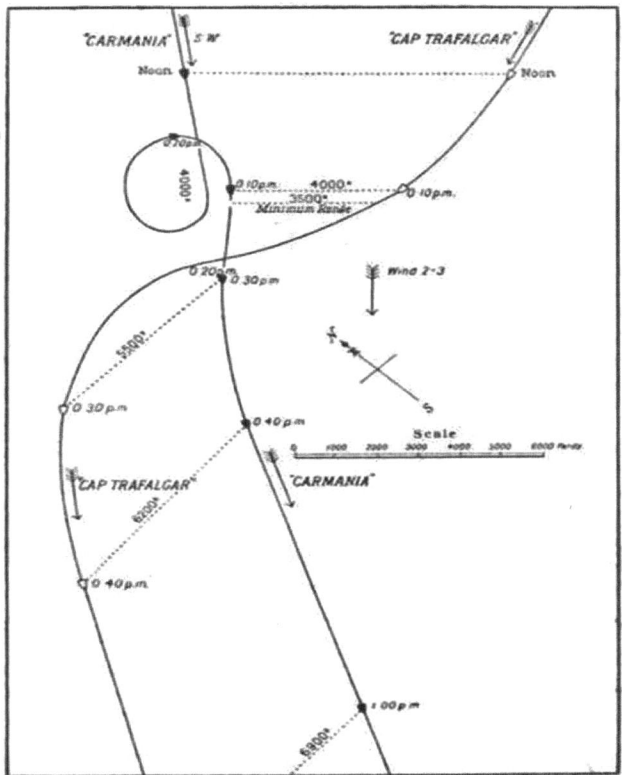

(Diagram of action between 'CARMANIA' and 'CAP TRAFALGAR'.)

One of his shells, however, had passed through the captain's cabin under the fore bridge, and although it did not burst it started a fire, which rapidly became worse; unhappily no water was available to put it out, for the fire main was shot through, while the chemical fire extinguishers proved of little use. All water had to be carried by hand, but luckily the fire was prevented from spreading over the ship by a steel bulkhead, together with an ordinary fire-proof swing door, which was afterwards found to be all charred on one side. Nevertheless it got a firm hold of the deck above, which broke into flame, so the fore-bridge had to be abandoned. The ship had now to be steered from the stern, and all orders had to be shouted down by megaphone both to the engine rooms and to this new steering position in the bowels of the ship, which was connected up and in operation in fifty-seven seconds! To reduce the effect of the fire the vessel was kept before the wind, which necessitated turning right round again, so that the fight resolved itself into a chase.

The action was continued by the gun-layers, the fire-control position being untenable due to the fire, so each gun had to be worked and fired independently under the direction of its own officer. Among the ammunition supply parties there had been several casualties and the officers, finding it impossible to "spot" the fall of the shell, owing to the flashes from the enemy's guns obscuring their view from so low an elevation, lent a hand in carrying the ammunition from the hoists to the guns. In these big liners the upper deck, where the guns are mounted, is approximately 70 feet above the holds, whence the ammunition has to be hoisted and then carried by hand to the guns—a particularly arduous task.

Crossing, as it were, the enemy was at this time well on the starboard bow, but firing was continued until the distance was over 9,000 yards, the maximum range of the *Carmania's* guns. Owing to his superior speed and a slight divergence between the courses, the distance was gradually increasing all the time, and at 1.30 he was out of range. His list had now visibly increased, and his speed began to diminish, probably on account of the inrush of water through his coaling ports. It was surmised that there had not been sufficient time to secure these properly, for he had evidently been coaling at the time she arrived upon the scene.

Towards the end the *Cap Trafalgar's* fire had begun to slacken, though one of her guns continued to fire to the last, in spite of the fact that she was out of range. It became patent that she was doomed, and her every movement was eagerly watched through field-glasses for some minutes by those not occupied in quenching the fire. Suddenly the great vessel heeled right over; her funnels being almost parallel to the surface of the sea, looked just like two gigantic cannon as they pointed towards the *Carmania*; an instant later she went down by the bows, the stern remaining poised in mid-air for a few seconds, and then she abruptly disappeared out of sight at 1.50 P.M., the duel having lasted an hour and forty minutes.

There were no two opinions about the good fight she had put up, and all were loud in their praise of the gallant conduct of the Germans.

One of the enemy's colliers was observed approaching this scene of desolation in order to pick up survivors, some of whom had got away from the sinking ship in her boats. The collier had been flying the United States ensign, evidently as a ruse, in the hope that the *Carmania* might be induced to let her pass without stopping her for examination. It was, however, impossible to interfere with her owing to the fire that was still raging in the fore part of the ship. This kept our men at work trying to get it under, and necessitated keeping the ship running before the wind, the direction of which did not permit of approaching the spot in order to attempt to pick up survivors.

Smoke was now seen away to the northward, and the signalman reported that he thought he could make out the funnels of a cruiser. As the *Cap Trafalgar*, before sinking, had been in wireless communication with some German vessel, it was apprehended that one might be coming to her assistance. As the *Carmania* was totally unfit for further action, it was deemed advisable to avoid the risk of another engagement, so she steamed off at full speed in a southerly direction.

As soon as the collier and all that remained of the wreckage of the *Cap Trafalgar* was lost to view the gallant Cunarder was turned to the northwestward in the direction of the anchorage. She was unseaworthy, nearly all her navigational instruments and all the communications to the engines were destroyed, making the steering and navigation of the ship difficult and uncertain. When wireless touch was established, the *Cornwall* was called up and asked to meet and escort her in. But as she had only just started coaling she asked the *Bristol* to take her place. The next day the *Bristol*, which was in the vicinity, took the *Carmania* along until relieved the same night by the *Cornwall*, which escorted her on to the base, where temporary repairs were effected.

One of the enemy's shells was found to have passed through three thicknesses of steel plating without exploding, but in spite of this it set fire to some bedding which caused the conflagration under the fore bridge. Where projectiles had struck solid iron, such as a winch, splinters of the latter were to be seen scattered in all directions. The ship was hit seventy-nine times, causing no fewer than 304 holes.

There were 38 casualties. Five men were killed outright, 4 subsequently died from wounds, 5 were seriously wounded and 22 wounded—most of the latter were only slightly injured. All the casualties occurred on deck, chiefly among the guns' crews and ammunition supply parties. No one below was touched, but a third of those employed on deck were hit.

The following remarks may be of interest, and are taken from the author's letters, written on September 16th, after having been shown over the *Carmania*:

"When I went on board this morning, I was greatly struck by the few fatal casualties considering the number of holes here, there, and everywhere.

Not a single part of the upper deck could be crossed without finding holes. A remarkable fact was that only one officer, Lieutenant Murray, R.N.R., was hurt or damaged in any way, although the officers were in the most exposed positions, and the enemy's point of aim appeared to be the fore bridge.

"They had only three active service ratings on board; some of the gunlayers were old men, pensioners from the Navy.

"One of the senior officers told me that the first few rounds made him feel 'a bit dickey,' but that after that he took no notice of the bigger shells, though, curiously enough, he thoroughly objected to the smaller pom-poms which were 'most irritating.' He added that the men fought magnificently, and that the firemen worked 'like hell.' As flames and smoke from the fire on deck descended to the stokeholds by the ventilators instead of cool air, the states of things down below may easily be imagined.

"One chronometer was found to be going in spite of the wooden box which contained it having been burnt.

"The deeds of heroism were many.

"I liked the story of the little bugler boy, who had no more to do once the action had commenced, so he stood by one of the guns refusing to go under cover. As the gun fired he shouted: 'That's one for the blighters!' And again: 'There's another for the beggars—go it!' smacking the gunshield the while with his hand.

"Again one of the gunlayers, who lost his hand and also one leg during the engagement, insisted upon being held up when the German ship sank, so as to be able to cheer. I talked to him, and he waggled his stump at me quite cheerily and said, 'It was well worth losing an arm for.'

"It is good to feel that the spirit of our forefathers is still active in time of need."

CHAPTER VI
THE ACTION OFF CORONEL

"Then let him roll
His galleons round the little Golden Hynde,
Bring her to bay, if he can, on the high seas,
Ring us about with thousands, we'll not yield,
I and my Golden Hynde, we will go down,
With flag still flying on the last stump left us
And all my cannon spitting the fires
Of everlasting scorn into his face."

— Alfred Noyes (*Drake*).

The wanderings of the German squadron in the Pacific have been briefly traced as far as Easter Island, where it arrived on October 12th, 1914, and found the *Dresden*. The *Leipzig*, which had been chased from pillar to post by British and Japanese cruisers, and succeeded in eluding them, joined up shortly after to the relief of the German Admiral.

The contractor at Easter Island, an Englishman named Edwards, who supplied the Germans with fresh meat and vegetables, was a ranch-owner, and had no idea that war had even been declared. One of his men, in taking off provisions to the ships, discovered this amazing fact, which had carefully been kept secret, and informed his master. The account was not settled in cash, but by a bill made payable at Valparaiso. The German squadron sailed for Mas-a-Fuera a week later, so the ranch-owner took the earliest opportunity of sending in his bill to Valparaiso, where it was duly honoured, vastly to his astonishment and relief.

For the reasons already adduced, it seemed almost certain that Admiral von Spee would make his way round South America. That there was a possibility of his descending upon Vancouver and attacking the naval dockyard of Esquimalt is acknowledged, but it was so remote as to be scarcely worthy of serious consideration. The three Japanese cruisers, *Idzuma, Hizen,* and *Asama*, were understood to be in the eastern Pacific at this time, and this was probably known to the German Admiral. The risk, too, that he must inevitably run in attacking a locality known to possess submarines was quite unjustifiable; besides, he had little to gain and everything to lose through the delay that must ensue from adopting such a policy.

The vessels engaged in the action off Coronel, with their armament, etc., were:[5]

Names	Tonnage	Armament	Speed	Completion
Good Hope	14,100	2—9.2"	23.5	1902
		16—6"		
Monmouth	9,800	14—6"	23.3	1903
Glasgow	4,800	2—6"	25.8	1910
		10—4"		
Otranto (armed liner)	12,000 gross	8—4.7"	18	1909
Speed of squadron 18 knots.				
Scharnhorst	11,420	8—8.2"	22.5	1908
		6—5.9"		
		20—3.4"		
Gneisenau	11,420	8—8.2"	23.8	1908
		6—5.9"		
		20—3.4"		
Leipzig	3,200	10—4.1"	23	1906
Dresden	3,544	12—4.1"	27	1908
		4—2.1"		
Nürnberg	3,396	10—4.1"	23.5	1908
		8—2.1"		

Speed of squadron 22.5 knots.

It will be noticed that our two armoured cruisers were respectively six and five years older than the Germans'. Our armament was much inferior in size, number, and quality on account of the later designs of the enemy's artillery. The range of the German 4.1-inch guns was *nearly equal to that of our 6-inch guns*. But perhaps the greatest point in favour of the enemy was the fact that Cradock's ships, with the exception of the *Glasgow*, were only commissioned at the outbreak of war, and had had such continuous steaming that no really good opportunity for gunnery practices or for testing the organisation thoroughly had been possible, whilst von Spee's had been in commission for over two years and had highly trained crews, accustomed to their ships.

The following account has been compiled from personal information received from officers who took part, from letters that have appeared in the Press, from a translation that has been published of Admiral von Spee's official report, and from the official report made by Captain Luce of the *Glasgow*.

Admiral Cradock, as we have seen, joined the remainder of his little squadron with the exception of the *Canopus* off the coast of Chile on October 29th. The latter was following at her best speed. The squadron proceeded northwards, whilst the *Glasgow* was detached to Coronel to send telegrams, a rendezvous being fixed for her to rejoin at 1 P.M. on November 1st.

No authentic news of the movements of the Germans was available at this time; in fact, the last time that von Spee's squadron had been definitely heard of was when it appeared off Papeete and bombarded the town toward the end of September. That the enemy might be encountered at any moment was of course fully realised, but it was hoped that either the *Dresden* and *Leipzig* or the main squadron might be brought to action separately, before they were able to join forces. Time was everything if this was to be brought about, so Admiral Cradock pushed on without delay. The anxiety to obtain news of a reliable character may be imagined, but only the vaguest of rumours, one contradicting the other, were forthcoming. Reports showed that the German merchant shipping in the neighbourhood were exhibiting unwonted signs of energy in loading coal and stores, but this gave no certain indication of the proximity of the entire squadron.

Rejoining the British squadron at sea on November 1st, the *Glasgow* communicated with the *Good Hope*. Our ships had recently been hearing Telefunken[6] signals on their wireless, which was proof that one or more enemy warships were close at hand. About 2 P.M., therefore, the Admiral signalled the squadron to spread on a line bearing N.E. by E. from the *Good Hope*, which steered N.W. by N. at 10 knots. Ships were ordered to open to a distance of fifteen miles apart at a speed of 15 knots, the *Monmouth* being nearest to the flagship, the *Otranto* next, and then the *Glasgow*, which was thus nearest the coast.

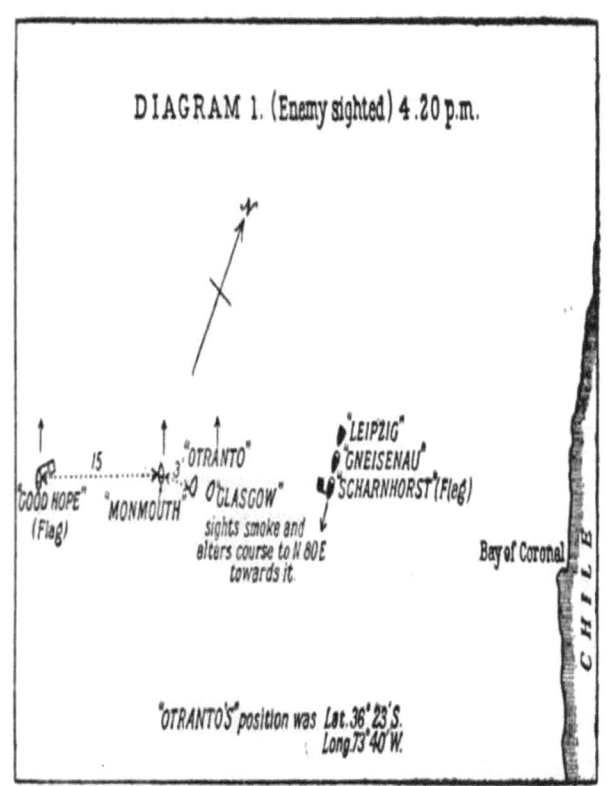

DIAGRAM I. (Enemy sighted) 4.20 p.m.

There was not sufficient time to execute this manœuvre, and when smoke was suddenly sighted at 4.20 P.M. to the eastward of the *Otranto* and *Glasgow*, these two ships were still close together and about four miles from the *Monmouth*. The *Glasgow* went ahead to investigate and made out three German warships, which at once turned towards her. The Admiral was over twenty miles, distant and out of sight, and had to be informed as soon as possible, so the *Glasgow* returned at full speed, warning him by wireless, which the Germans endeavoured to jam, that the enemy was in sight.

The squadron reformed at full speed on the flagship, *who had altered course to the southward*, and by 5.47 P.M. had got into single line-ahead in the order: *Good Hope, Monmouth, Glasgow,* and *Otranto*. The enemy, in similar formation, was about twelve miles off.

For the better understanding of the movements which follow, it may be stated that the ideal of a naval artillerist is a good target — that is, a clear and well defined object which is plainly visible through the telescopic gunsights; the wind in the right direction, relative to the engaged side, so that smoke does not blow across the guns, and no sudden alterations of course, to throw out calculations. The tactics of a modern naval action are in a large measure based on these ideals, at any rate according to the view of the gunnery specialist.

It is evident that it was Admiral Cradock's intention to close in and force action at short range as quickly as possible, in order that the enemy might be handicapped by the rays of the lowering sun, which would have been behind our ships, rendering them a very poor target for the Germans as the squadrons drew abeam of one another. He therefore altered course inwards towards the enemy, but von Spee was either too wary or too wise, for he says in his report that he turned away to a southerly course after 5.35, thus declining action, which the superior speed of his squadron enabled him to do at his pleasure. The wind was south (right ahead), and it was blowing very fresh, so that a heavy head sea was encountered, which made all ships—especially the light-cruisers—pitch and roll considerably. It seems very doubtful whether the *Good Hope* and *Monmouth* were able to use their main deck guns, and it is certain that they could not have been of any value. This would mean that these two ships could only fire two 9.2-inch and ten 6-inch guns on the broadside between them, instead of their whole armament of two 9.2-inch and seventeen 6-inch guns.

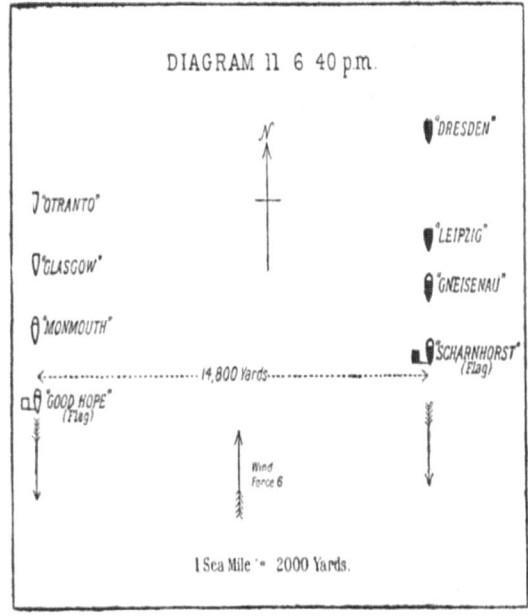

DIAGRAM II 6.40 p.m.

There was little daylight left when Admiral Cradock tried to close the Germans, hoping that they would accept his challenge in view of their superior strength.

At 6.18 Admiral Cradock increased speed to 17 knots, making a wireless message to the *Canopus*, "I am about to attack enemy now." Both squadrons were now on parallel courses approximately, steering south, and about 7½ miles apart. A second light cruiser joined the German line about this period; according to von Spee's report the *Scharnhorst* was leading, followed by the *Gneisenau, Leipzig,* and *Dresden*.

As the sun sank below the horizon (about 6.50 P.M.) the conditions of light became reversed to our complete disadvantage; our ships were now lit up by the glow of the sunset, the enemy being gradually enshrouded in a misty haze as the light waned. Admiral Cradock's last hope of averting defeat must have vanished as he watched the enemy turning away; at the best he could only expect to damage and thus delay the enemy, while it was impossible to withdraw. He had no choice but to hold on and do his best, trusting in Providence to aid him. In judging what follows it should be kept in mind that in the declining light even the outlines of the enemy's ships rapidly became obliterated, making it quite impossible to see the fall of our shots in order to correct the range on the gunsights; on the other hand, our ships showed up sharply against the western horizon and still provided good targets for the German gunners. Von Spee in his report says his "guns' crews on the middle decks were never able to see the sterns of their opponents, and only occasionally their bows." This certainly implies that the upper deck gunners could see quite well, whilst we have information from Captain Luce's report that our ships were unable to see the enemy early in the action, and were firing at the flashes of his guns.

Accordingly, as soon as the sun disappeared, von Spee lost no time in approaching our squadron, and opened fire at 7.4 at a range of 12,000 yards. Our ships at once followed suit with the exception of the *Otranto*, whose old guns did not admit of her competing against men-of-war at this distance. The German Admiral apparently endeavoured to maintain this range, so as to reap the full advantage of his newer and heavier armament, for the two 9.2-inch guns in the *Good Hope* were the only ones in the whole of our squadron that were effective at this distance with the possible exception of the two modern 6-inch guns in the *Glasgow*. Von Spee had, of course, calculated this out, and took care not to close until our armoured cruisers were *hors de combat*.

The Germans soon found the range, their fire proving very accurate, which was to be expected in view of the reputation of the *Scharnhorst* and

Gneisenau for good shooting—the former had won the gold medal for the best average. These armoured cruisers concentrated their fire entirely on our two leading ships, doing considerable execution. In addition, they had a great stroke of luck, for in the first ten minutes of the engagement a shell struck the fore turret of the *Good Hope*, putting that 9.2-inch out of action. The *Monmouth* was apparently hit several times in rapid succession, for she was forced to haul out of the line to the westward, and her forecastle was seen to be burning furiously, but she continued to return the enemy's fire valiantly. This manœuvre caused her to drop astern, and compelled the *Glasgow*, who now followed on after the *Good Hope*, to ease speed to avoid getting into the zone of fire intended for the *Monmouth*.

It was now growing dark, but this did not deter both squadrons from continuing to blaze away as hard as they could; in fact, the fight was at its height; the German projectiles were falling all round and about our ships, causing several fires which lit them up with a ghostly hue. The heavy artillery of the enemy was doing great damage, and it was evident that both the *Good Hope* and *Monmouth* were in a bad way; the former sheered over unsteadily towards the Germans, returning their fire spasmodically, whilst the latter had a slight list and from her erratic movements gave the impression that her steering arrangements had been damaged. The results of our shooting could not be distinguished with accuracy, though von Spee mentions that the *Scharnhorst* found a 6-inch shell in one of her storerooms, which had penetrated the side and caused a deal of havoc below but did not burst, and also that one funnel was hit. The *Gneisenau* had two men wounded, and sustained slight damage.

At 7.50 P.M. a sight of the most appalling splendour arrested everyone, as if spellbound, in his tussle with death. An enormous sheet of flame suddenly burst from the *Good Hope*, lighting up the whole heavens for miles around. This was accompanied by the noise of a terrific explosion, which hurled up wreckage and sparks at least a couple of hundred feet in the air from her after funnels. A lucky shot had penetrated one of her magazines. "It reminded me of Vesuvius in eruption," said a seaman in describing this spectacle. It was now pitch dark, making it impossible for the opposing vessels to distinguish one another. The *Good Hope* was never heard to fire her guns again, and could not have long survived such a terrible explosion, though no one saw her founder.

The moon had risen about 6.30 P.M. and was now well up, but it was too overcast to see much. According to von Spee the squadrons had closed in to about 5,400 yards, which caused him to sheer off, fearing torpedo attack. It seems certain that although firing was continued it could not have been effective, for three minutes after the *Good Hope* blew up the Germans ceased fire altogether. Shortly afterwards von Spee ordered the *Leipzig*, *Dresden*, and *Nürnberg*—the last-named having joined the squadron during the action—to make a torpedo attack.

The *Monmouth* ceased firing just before the explosion on board the *Good Hope*, and was then steering roughly N.W. It was clear she was on her last legs, as her list had increased and she was down by the bows. She now suddenly altered course to the N.E. in the direction of the oncoming enemy. Captain Luce was senior naval officer, being senior to Captain Brandt, of the *Monmouth*. He saw the Germans approaching and signalled the *Monmouth* at 8.30, "Enemy following us," but received no reply. Clearly there was no alternative left him but to save his ship, if he was not to make a needless sacrifice of his men, as it was obvious that he could be of no further assistance to his doomed consort. In addition, it was essential that the *Canopus* should be warned in time to avert a further calamity, a task not so simple as it sounds, for the Germans were jamming our wireless messages. It is said that when last seen the gallant *Monmouth* turned and made straight for the enemy in a heroic attempt to ram one of their ships. Von Spee reports that the *Nürnberg* sank the *Monmouth* at 9.28 P.M. by bombardment at point-blank range; this accounts for the seventy-five flashes of gunfire as well as the play of the beams of a search-light, which were observed by the *Glasgow* after leaving the scene of action. It must have been brutal work.

Thus perished Admiral Cradock together with 1,600 gallant officers and men. In fairness to the Germans it should be stated that our own officers considered it too rough for boats to be lowered with any safety.

The *Glasgow* had been subjected to the combined fire of the *Leipzig* and *Dresden*, whose gunnery was fortunately not very effective owing to the long range maintained between the two squadrons before the light failed. That she had withstood this combined onslaught for fifty-two minutes (von Spee's report) was remarkable, but that she had suffered no material damage was little short of a miracle. Her casualties amounted to four men slightly wounded. She was hit five times, on or near the water line, but not in vital places. The protection afforded by the coal in her bunkers saved her on three occasions, as otherwise in the nasty sea running at the time she would have found herself in a very precarious position. Of the remaining two hits, one penetrated the deck but did not explode, while the other wrecked the captain's pantry and cabin. There was one large hole, which luckily did not prevent her eluding her pursuers at high speed by steering out to the W.N.W., and thence in a wide circle to the southward to the Magellan Straits, finally arriving at Port Stanley in the Falkland Islands.

At the outset of the engagement the *Good Hope* made a signal down the line to the *Otranto*, the only words received being, "Leaving *Otranto*." The latter, therefore, hauled out to endeavour to get this signal direct from the flagship, but as the *Good Hope* had been badly hit, nothing further was received. As projectiles were falling all round her, and it was realised that the *Otranto*, being a large ship, would be used by the enemy as a rangefinder to enable him to calculate the distance of the *Glasgow*, she hauled out still farther to upset the accuracy of his gun-fire. The enemy proceeded to carry this method of ranging into effect; the first salvo passed over the *Otranto's* bridge, the second missed the bows by 50 yards, the third fell 150 yards astern, while others which followed fell, some over, some short. By this time she had worked out of the line about 1,200 yards, so turned to the same course, as far as could be judged, as the remainder of the squadron. She was now out of range. The *Otranto* ran the gauntlet of the enemy's most successfully, since she emerged from this storm of shell quite unscathed, but it must have been touch and go. Moreover—and hardest of all—she had to submit to this treatment without being in a position to retaliate. After the flagship blew up, nothing was seen of the *Monmouth*; subsequently the *Glasgow* was reported crossing her stern. Seeing that she could be of no assistance, the *Otranto* dodged her opponents by straining full speed to the westward for 200 miles, and thence to the southward. Rounding Cape Horn, she passed between the Falklands and the mainland and arrived at Montevideo. Both she and the *Glasgow* must have accounted themselves most fortunate in escaping safely from this unequal contest.

The *Canopus*, which had been steaming northward with two colliers, intercepted a wireless message from the *Glasgow* to the *Good Hope* reporting the enemy in sight. She immediately increased to her full speed, dispatching the colliers to Juan Fernandez, and proceeded on her course northward in the hope that she would arrive in time to engage the enemy. About 9 P.M. she received a signal from the *Glasgow* that it was feared the *Good Hope* and *Monmouth* had been sunk, and that the squadron was scattered. Seeing the hopelessness of continuing on her course, the *Canopus* turned round, picked up her colliers, and made for the Magellan Straits via Smyth's Channel, the successful navigation of which reflects great credit, since she was probably the first battleship ever to make use of it. By this means she succeeded in reaching Port Stanley without molestation, although the German ships were constantly in close proximity.

Admiral Cradock appears to have had definite orders to prevent the enemy coming round to the east coast of America. The *Canopus* was only 120 miles away when he met the enemy. But had the Admiral waited for her the Germans might have slipped past him during the night, and, moreover, her slow speed would have seriously hampered the mobility of his squadron. Speaking of Admiral Cradock, Sir Henry Newbolt[7] says, "He had asked for reinforcements, and the Admiralty had sent him what they thought sufficient. It was not for him to hold back."

The advantages of speed and modern guns of superior range were perhaps the outstanding features of the Coronel action. It was not the vain sacrifice which at first sight it might appear to be, as it probably saved our ships operating on the east coast of South America from a similar fate.

Admiral Cradock carried out unflinchingly his search for a force which he knew would almost certainly be superior to his own. His unhesitating acceptance of the action and the gallantry of the fight uphold the finest traditions of the Royal Navy, and will always be recalled by it with pride. Surely, before God and man, such deeds of heroism go far to mitigate the infamy of war.

"At set of sun,
Even as below the sea-line the broad disc
Sank like a red-hot cannon-ball through surf
Of seething molten lead, the *Santa Maria*,
Uttering one cry that split the heart of heaven,
Went down with all hands, roaring into the dark."

Alfred Noyes (*Drake*).

CHAPTER VII
CONCENTRATION

"And Drake growled, ...
... 'So, lest they are not too slow
To catch us, clear the decks. God, I would like
To fight them!'"

—Alfred Noyes (*Drake*).

Several disquieting wireless messages were received by the British warships on the east coast of South America, giving garbled and unreliable accounts of the Coronel action. It was not till November 5th that a statement which appeared to be fairly authoritative, in spite of its German origin, was received from Valparaiso. It said that the *Monmouth* was sunk and that the *Good Hope* had probably shared her fate; no mention was made of the *Canopus*, *Glasgow*, or *Otranto*.

The command in these waters now devolved upon Rear-Admiral Stoddart (flying his flag in the *Carnarvon*), who was still busily engaged in the search for the *Karlsruhe*. His ships had been operating over a wide area extending from the neighbourhood of Rio de Janeiro to the northward of St. Paul's Rocks and the Rocas, and thence to the westward along the north coast of South America. This otherwise fruitless search achieved one notable result in compelling the *Karlsruhe* to abandon her system of obtaining supplies through German storeships coming from Pernambuco, as that port was kept under rigid observation. She was thus forced to leave the trade route between Great Britain and South America for longer periods in order to meet her consort, the armed liner *Kronprinz Wilhelm*, who now became a link between her and her sources of supply in Central America. There was, in consequence, a marked falling off at this period in the number of her captures.

Assuming that the worst had happened, and that the German squadron was now on its way round to the east coast, it became imperative to unite our remaining ships into one squadron as quickly as possible. It was obvious that with the Australian and Japanese ships behind them, the

Germans could not afford to linger where they were; moreover, they had learned at Valparaiso that we had no naval force of any preponderance with which to oppose them. Flushed with their recent victory, it seemed probable that if they were not much damaged they would most likely hasten their movements in the hope of meeting our ships before we had had time to unite or to gather reinforcements.

The German squadron would not be able to separate with any safety once we had succeeded in joining together our scattered forces, so that the damage they might do to our commerce would be thereby reduced to a minimum.

For these reasons it will be seen that the River Plate was admirably situated for the rendezvous of our ships that had escaped from Coronel to the Falklands, and of the northern squadron. Again, it was possible to coal there without infringing territorial rights, as there is an excellent anchorage well outside the three mile limit from the foreshore.

The following calculations, written on November 6th, 1914, were made by the author:

"The German Admiral will expect us to get reinforcements out from England, so that it seems probable that he will lose no time in coming round to the east coast.

"He arrived at Valparaiso on November 3rd. Supposing he coals there and leaves at earliest on November 4th, the distance from Valparaiso to the Plate is roughly 2,600 miles, or nine days at 12 knots; therefore, allowing one day for coaling *en route*, the earliest that he could be off the Plate would be the 13th, more likely not before November 15th."

The strategical aspect in this sphere of operations was completely changed by the success of the German squadron off Cape Coronel, and necessitated not only a complete change of plans, but also an entire redistribution of our ships. These consisted of the *Carnarvon, Cornwall, Bristol, Macedonia,* and *Edinburgh Castle,* also the *Defence* and *Orama,* who were near Montevideo, and the *Canopus, Glasgow,* and *Otranto.*

Admiral Stoddart, therefore, decided to go south to Montevideo at once in order to meet the remainder of our scattered ships. The *Bristol, Macedonia,* and *Edinburgh Castle* were left to continue the search for the *Karlsruhe,* although as a matter of fact she had blown up on November 4th. Colliers were sent down south to Montevideo to be in readiness for our ships, and were ordered to sail at twelve-hour intervals to diminish the chance of capture.

The *Carnarvon* and *Cornwall* left the base on November 6th, the former calling at Rio de Janeiro on the way for telegrams. Arriving at the Plate on the 10th, where we found the *Defence* and *Orama*, the Admiral immediately transferred his flag to the former ship, which was the newest and most powerful of our cruisers. All ships filled up with coal and awaited the arrival of the *Glasgow* and *Otranto*; meanwhile, patrols were constantly maintained at the mouth of the river.

The following evening the *Glasgow* arrived amidst congratulations from us all; she had put in to the Falkland Islands to coal, in which assistance was provided by volunteers from amongst the inhabitants. After coaling, she was detached to Rio de Janeiro to go into dry dock, so that the damage to her side might be properly repaired. The same day the *Orama*, whilst patrolling, met and sank the German storeship *Navarra* which was set on fire by the Germans when escape was seen to be impossible. We also got the cheering news that the *Emden* had been sunk and that the *Königsberg* had been bottled up, tidings which augured well for the future.

The Admiralty seem to have had a premonition that the Germans intended to attack the Falklands for the *Canopus*, although on her way north to Montevideo, was ordered back to the Falkland Islands in order to fortify and arm the harbour of Port Stanley in co-operation with the local volunteers, converting herself into a floating fort.

The possibility of our encountering and having to fight von Spee was the subject uppermost in all minds at this time, and led to a great deal of discussion. The outstanding feature in the situation was the extraordinary lack of homogeneity of the composition of our squadron. It consisted of three armoured cruisers of entirely different classes, each carrying a different armament, one light cruiser and four armed merchantmen. The latter could not, of course, be pitted against warships even of the light-cruiser type, and therefore had to be left out of the reckoning. Amongst the four fighting ships there were four descriptions of guns, viz. two 9.2-inch, fourteen 7.5-inch, twenty-two 6-inch, and ten 4-inch, while the German squadron had only three descriptions, viz. sixteen 8.2-inch, twelve 5.9-inch, and thirty-two 4.1-inch. A prominent question, therefore, was what range we should endeavour to maintain during an action; the answer to which was very varied, preference being given to ranges from 14,000 yards downwards. From the gunnery point of view the enemy undoubtedly held an advantage, as not only was his squadron more homogeneous, having only two classes of ships, but also the range of his guns was greater. As regards speed, there was nothing to choose between the two squadrons, who were evenly matched in this respect. Much would depend upon whether he would choose to keep his squadron together for the purpose of an action or to disperse them on reaching the east coast. Opinions on this and on many other points were divided. All were agreed, however, that we ought to give a good account of ourselves.

The wildest reports about von Spee's movements were constantly received from Chilean and other sources. Whilst at Montevideo rumours were circulated that the German ships had been seen coming round Cape Horn.

The Admiralty now informed Admiral Stoddart that reinforcements were being sent out from England at once; they had actually started just after our arrival at the Plate. The secret of this news was well kept, not an inkling leaking out at home or abroad—a fact which contributed very largely to our subsequent victory. It was decided, therefore, to return northwards in order to effect a junction with the two battle-cruisers that were on their way out. The squadron sailed on November 12th, spread out in line abreast, and put in some useful exercises on the way. Arriving at the base five days later, we found the *Kent*, which was expected as we had heard that she was being sent out to reinforce us; she had brought a mail, which made her doubly welcome. The *Bristol* and *Edinburgh Castle* rejoined, but the latter was ordered off northwards on other service, and sailed on November 19th, taking a mail for England. It was blazing hot, but the next few days passed quickly enough in carrying out gunnery practices, patrolling, and coaling ship, during which the *Glasgow* returned from Rio, spick and span.

Most of November was a time of some suspense for our ships, as we were hourly expecting an encounter with the enemy, and it was with mixed feelings that we learned of the nature of the reinforcements that were coming out with such despatch. Our feelings of relief were also tempered with regret at not having been afforded an opportunity to prove our mettle. Further, there was an awful and terrible thought that it might be considered necessary to leave one of us cruisers behind to guard the base.

Most of our ships had had steam on their main engines incessantly since war broke out, and a rest to let fires out so as to make necessary adjustments was badly needed, but was quite impossible near a neutral coast.

On November 26th our hearts were gladdened by the sight of the *Invincible*, bearing the flag of Vice-Admiral Sturdee, and the *Inflexible*; these two formidable-looking ships had come out from England at a mean speed of over 18 knots for fifteen days. Truly a fine performance!

CHAPTER VIII
POSSIBILITIES AND PROBABILITIES

The various possible courses open to Admiral Count von Spee, both before and after Coronel, have already been discussed, but the movements of his squadron have not been subjected to examination in the light that they bear on the policy which he adopted, nor have the results of that action been considered from his point of view.

The German squadron sailed from Mas-a-Fuera on October 27th, and three days later arrived about noon at a position some fifty miles to the westward of Valparaiso, where it remained for upwards of twenty-four hours. On October 31st—the same day that the *Glasgow* went into Coronel with telegrams and the day before that action was fought—the squadron steamed off south, leaving the *Nürnberg* to wait off Valparaiso for a few hours and probably to get information of importance. The German Admiral undoubtedly went to the neighbourhood of Valparaiso with the express intention of obtaining news and was in communication with the shore, for he begins his official report on the action fought off Coronel by saying that his three light cruisers reached on November 1st a point about twenty "sea miles from the Chilean coast, in order to attack a British cruiser (*Glasgow*), which, according to trustworthy information, had reached the locality on the previous evening."

It is, of course, impossible to know what were von Spee's intentions at this moment; they can only be surmised from a general survey of the situation and the means that he had of obtaining information. The latter was acquired by an organised system, for there were German agents in every South American port. It may be taken as certain that any ship calling at or passing Punta Arenas (Magellan Straits) would be reported to him, and that the names of the ships and certain of their movements on the south-east coast would also be known to him.

Easter Island—which was von Spee's original base—is approximately 2,300 miles from Valparaiso, and therefore out of range of wireless communication, although it is possible he might occasionally be able to take in a message under favourable conditions. However, it is known from an officer survivor of the *Gneisenau* that on October 19th the German Admiral received a message—possibly through a German supply ship—stating that a British Squadron consisting of "*Good Hope, Monmouth,* and *Glasgow* was to the south." Now we know that this squadron was at Punta Arenas on September 28th, and leaving on that date was employed searching inlets and bays round Tierra del Fuego for some days. The *Good Hope* then returned to the Falklands, finally leaving them on October 22nd, whilst the others went on to the coast of Chile and were there from October 11th onwards, making use of a sequestered spot as a base. The *Glasgow* was at Coronel on October 14th and at Valparaiso the day following, so the fact of a British Squadron being "south" was well known, though the information did not reach von Spee till the 19th.

On receiving this news von Spee sailed immediately. He knew he was in superior force to Cradock's squadron, and the presumption is that he went over to prospect and, if possible, to force an action. He went straight to Mas-a-Fuera, only remained two days to coal, and then on to a position off Valparaiso to pick up further information.

Immediately on hearing that the *Glasgow* was at Coronel on the 31st, he proceeded south to cut her off, and, as was likely to be the case, to meet Cradock. He must have judged that the rest of the squadron could not be far behind the *Glasgow*. The probability was that he received information of the *Good Hope* passing through the Straits about the 24th or 25th, and he might also have heard of the *Canopus* doing so a day or two later, in which case he would have calculated that the latter could scarcely be so far north by this time.

There is no indication that by this date von Spee had made up his mind to quit the South Pacific. He had hardly had time to make his arrangements for so doing, and there is no doubt that they were not then completed.

Von Spee was at his full strength, having recently added the *Dresden* and *Leipzig* to the squadron while at Easter Island, he possessed the advantage of homogeneity, and his squadron was far more modern. The result we know, our ships were out-gunned and completely outclassed. Fate played right into the hands of von Spee on this occasion.

It was undoubtedly a severe blow to British prestige in these parts, and the Germans in all the large towns were not slow in making the most of this temporary success in order to advance their own interests. The rumours that were circulated caused no little perturbation amongst the neutral shipping agents, who feared that von Spee would lose no time in attacking British trade, and that those cargoes which were consigned to Great Britain would be in jeopardy. Insurance rates rose with a bound, and it is said that the Germans went about openly deriding the British and causing the most fantastic articles to be inserted in the local Press. The exaggerated reports that were published, both of the action and of its effects, certainly lends colour to this source of information.

It will be interesting to consider what von Spee would have done if he had missed Admiral Cradock and the action off Coronel had not been fought. In view of his superior speed, von Spee would in all probability have continued on his southerly course and rounded Cape Horn, leaving Admiral Cradock behind him. There seem to be grounds for supposing that he might go to the Cape of Good Hope, but the campaign in German South West Africa could scarcely be said to be progressing favourably for the Germans, and it is not unreasonable to suppose he would have preferred to go north along the eastern side of South America to harass our trade. It is legitimate to suppose that in this case he would not have delayed to attack the Falkland Islands, with Cradock's squadron on his heels and Stoddart's ships converging on him from the north; in fact, it would have been suicidal, for the wireless station there would have given our ships warning of his approach, and the delay might have enabled our two forces to unite. From Stoddart's squadron alone he had nothing to fear, and most likely would have welcomed an opportunity of bringing it to action. The presence of the *Defence* at Montevideo would certainly have been known to him at that time, and he would probably have hoped to intercept her before she joined Cradock. Had all this come to pass, the Germans might then have separated, and when it was found that the theatre of operations in the South Atlantic became too hot for them, they might have endeavoured to make their way home after doing as much damage as possible to our commerce.

As events turned out, however, von Spee waited about at sea for a day or two after the action, apparently in the hope of either hearing news of the *Good Hope* or finding her. Writing at sea on November 2nd, he says, in a letter that afterwards appeared in the German Press: "If *Good Hope* escaped, she must, in my opinion, make for a Chilean port on account of her damages. To make sure of this, I intend going to Valparaiso to-morrow with *Gneisenau* and *Nürnberg*, and to see whether *Good Hope* could not be disarmed by the Chileans." Writing under date of November 5th, he adds: "We arrived at Valparaiso this morning.... The news of our victory had not yet reached here, but spread very quickly." The squadron split up, it seems, arriving at different dates at Mas-a-Fuera, which became the temporary headquarters of the German squadron for the next fortnight. Here all ships coaled in turn. Communication was maintained by sending the German light cruisers into Valparaiso one after the other to get the latest information. The *Leipzig* was there somewhere about November 13th. This would show a proper caution on his part, as belligerent vessels cannot use neutral ports except at extended intervals.

At Valparaiso von Spee must have obtained information concerning the movements of our squadron under Admiral Stoddart, who had then just sailed north from Montevideo. He would also have probably been aware of the presence of the Japanese squadron operating in the Northern Pacific.

In order to make the position clear, it must be apprehended that a squadron consisting of the British light cruiser *Newcastle*, together with the Japanese cruiser *Idzuma*, and the small battleship *Hizen*, was concentrated in the North Pacific. The battle-cruiser *Australia* left Suva, Fiji, on November 8th to strengthen this squadron, so that it may be deduced that this was a direct result of the Coronel action which took place just a week before. She joined these ships on November 26th at Chamela Bay on the west coast of Mexico. The object of this squadron was to prevent von Spee from coming north, and to close on him should he remain on the western coast of South America. Sailing southwards, these ships visited the Galapagos Islands and then proceeded on their quest for the enemy, the *Newcastle* searching the Cocos Islands *en route*. When nearing the coast of Colombia, the splendid news of the Falkland Islands battle was received, after which these ships split up and separated.

In view of these various courses of action open to von Spee, the reader will appreciate how our minds were occupied with the question of his future movements. Would he, in the hope of adding further to his laurels, attempt to repeat his success by going into the North Pacific to engage the Allied squadron there, which might have been inferior to him in strength? Or would he go south and follow up his advantage in a direction where there was nothing to oppose him for the moment, except the *Canopus* and *Glasgow*? He could not hope successfully to combat all the different squadrons looking for him, nor, for that matter, did he wish to risk his ships, for there were no others to replace them. It was not his rôle to adopt such an offensive. He therefore chose to give the impression that he was remaining off Chile, and then suddenly vanished into complete oblivion. Leaving no trace of his movements, he was careful to forgo using all wireless; and, having completed arrangements as to future supplies, he determined to appear suddenly where he was least expected. History repeats itself, and he evidently decided that the boldest plan was what would be least anticipated, and therefore most likely to be productive of success.

Taking another point of view, it was obviously to von Spee's advantage to hasten round to the east coast of South America as quickly as possible after the action off Coronel took place, and thus to reap the full benefit of the success that he had already gained. He could not possibly have shut his eyes to the fact that the immediate following up of his victory was the most promising policy for any scheme of operations in the South Atlantic. He would then have been able to strike before reinforcements could come out from England, which he must have been aware would be sent out to hunt him down. Why, then, did he delay a whole month? On his own showing the repairs necessary to render his ships fit for further service only took a few days, and it would not take long to arrange for his future supplies on the east coast of South America with all the German shipping cooped up in this part of the world waiting to be put to any useful purpose. Is it, therefore, unreasonable to suppose that he waited in order to collect German reservists from Chile, either to garrison the Falkland Islands once they had been captured, or to take or escort them home to Germany? He knew that he was really superior to the force under Admiral Stoddart, yet he delayed leaving till November 26th, a period of nearly four weeks. The inference of which is that he was not ready, and further that a seizure of the Falkland Islands was deliberately contemplated and prepared for, and was to be his first step. An additional possible explanation lies in the deduction that he could not have estimated that he would have defeated Cradock so completely, and therefore took time to consider the altered situation before committing himself to a definite move, hoping in the interval to get more information which might lead to a further stroke of good fortune. The threat of the *Australia* and the Japanese squadron to the north was not sufficiently pronounced to force him to hurry.

We have seen that it was almost out of the question for von Spee to maintain his ships in the Northern Pacific, but the conditions were entirely different on the west coast of South America. Here there were a number of uninhabited anchorages where he could shelter, and he had a large German population to help him on the coast of Chile. In fact, he did maintain himself here until he knew that hostile forces were concentrating and would move south to drive him out. Meanwhile, he had effected repairs to his ships, and had completed arrangements in advance for the supplies of his ships on the east coast of South America. Thus the conclusion appeared to be that there was no alternative open to von Spee but to leave the Pacific, where he had already shot his bolt.

Whatever the true explanation of his policy may be, the movements of his squadron point to his having been quite at a loss what to do next. His position was so hazardous and uncertain, so full of future difficulties, that he could not see his way clear for any length of time in order to work out any concerted plan. He was a fugitive pure and simple, and felt that whatever he did was in the nature of a venture.

It was not till Cradock was defeated that he appears to have formulated his plan for attacking the Falkland Islands. He then seems to have been carried away by the effect that the temporary capture of a British colony and the hoisting of the German flag would have on our prestige throughout the world. He would have destroyed the wireless station, seized the coal and provisions lying there, and would then have had to abandon the colony to subsequent recapture. Had he originally contemplated such a dramatic coup, he would never have delayed a moment longer than was necessary.

Keeping well away from the usual trade routes, the German ships sailed south, and on the way were lucky enough to meet the *North Wales*, one of Cradock's colliers. They arrived at San Quintin Sound on November 21st, coaled, and stayed five days. Thence von Spee kept out for 200 miles from the land before turning south, and got into very rough weather.

An officer in the *Gneisenau* states:

"*November 27th*—Force of wind up to 12. Later the weather moderated a little so that we could proceed at 8 knots.

"*November 29th*—Impossible to lay the tables. Broken up furniture thrown overboard. All crockery was smashed. Impossible to be on deck. Necessary to secure oneself with ropes. We are about off the entrance to the Magellan Straits.

"*December 2nd*—Sighted two icebergs, appear to be 50 metres high.

"*December 3rd*—We are lying at the eastern exit of the Beagle Channel close to Picton Island.

"*December 6th*—We are going to Port Stanley."

In judging von Spee's motives, it is as well to bear in mind that he attained no success whatsoever after Coronel except for the capture of two sailing ships and a collier. That our squadron under Admiral Sturdee, having only arrived the day previously, met him on his arrival off Port Stanley, was the turn of Fortune's wheel in our favour.

As all the world now knows, the battle of Coronel, the greatest naval disaster that had befallen our arms in the war, was to be avenged five weeks afterwards, when the German squadron in its turn drank to the dregs the bitter cup of despair.

Part II
THE BATTLE OF THE FALKLANDS

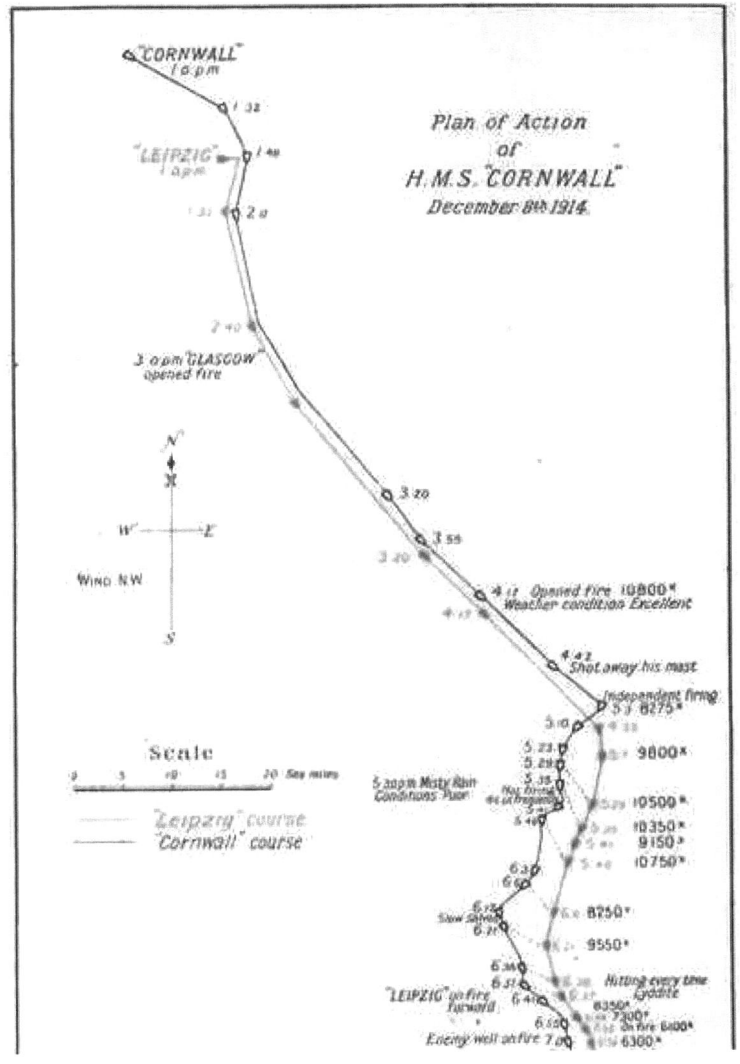

Plan of Action of H.M.S. "CORNWALL" December 8th 1914.

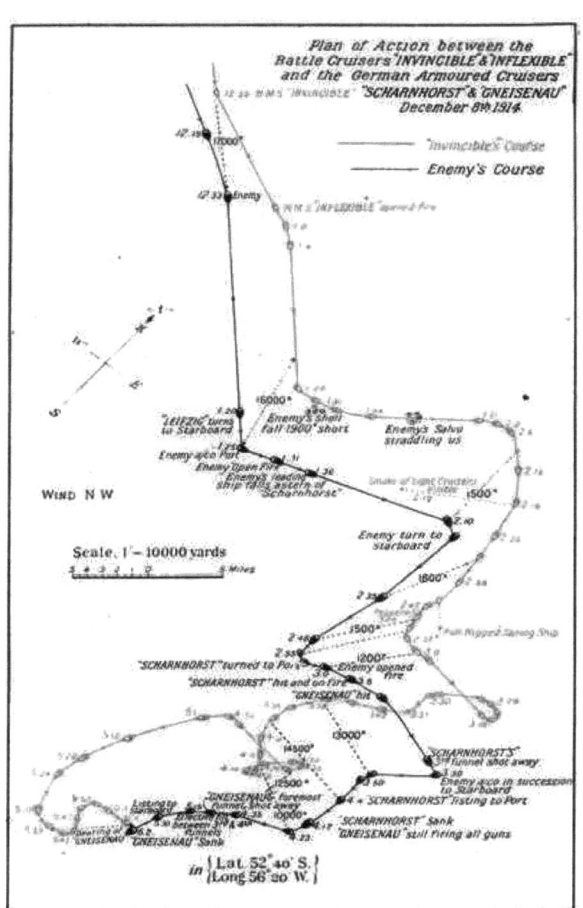

Plan of Action between the Battle Cruisers "INVINCIBLE" & "INFLEXIBLE" and the German Armoured Cruisers "SCHARNHORST" & "GNEISENAU" December 8th 1914.

CHAPTER IX
AWAY SOUTH

"Into the golden West, across the broad
Atlantic once again. 'For I will show,'
Said Drake, 'that Englishmen henceforth will sail
Old ocean where they will.'"

—Alfred Noyes (*Drake*).

The two battle-cruisers looked very businesslike as they steamed up to the anchorage; their trip out had taken off a good deal of paint, and they presented something of the appearance of hardened warriors returning from a spell in the trenches, as has been so well portrayed by Captain Bruce Bairnsfather. To our joy they brought a small mail only three weeks old.

No sooner had the rattle of their cables ceased than preparations for coaling were seen to be in progress.

The same day, November 26th, the *Defence* sailed for Cape Town via St. Helena to join the flag of Rear-Admiral H. G. King-Hall. The *Macedonia* and *Otranto* had been sent to Sierra Leone some time previously to let out fires and examine boilers.

The British Squadron was now under the command of Vice-Admiral F. C. D. Sturdee, who held the title of Commander-in-Chief, South Atlantic and Pacific. The Admiral's plan of operations possessed the distinctive feature of every good invention; it was extremely simple when once understood. Roughly speaking, it was this. The squadron was to sail south to the Falklands, spreading out to extreme visual signalling distance and searching for the enemy's ships. All signals were to be made by searchlight, and wireless was not to be used unless it was absolutely necessary. The battle-cruisers were placed in the centre of the squadron, comparatively close together, with the double object of being able to concentrate quickly in any direction and of keeping secret their presence in these waters. Orders were subsequently given that, after coaling at the Falklands, the squadron would leave on December 9th, "in order to get round the Horn before the enemy comes East." The enemy was sure to be reported if he used the Straits of Magellan; but it is believed that, to make doubly sure of not missing him, the Admiral intended to divide our squadron. Some of the cruisers would then have gone through the Straits, meeting him with the battle-cruisers somewhere in the Pacific; by this means the presence of the latter would not become known.

Sailing on November 28th, on a lovely calm morning, Admiral Sturdee must have indeed felt a proud man; after years of labour in his profession, he had his ambition realised by the command of a powerful squadron in war with a definite task before him. It consisted of *Invincible* (flag), *Inflexible*, *Carnarvon* (flag), *Cornwall*, *Kent*, *Glasgow*, and *Bristol*. The *Macedonia*, now on her way back from Sierra Leone, was to join us on the voyage south.

On December 1st a report was received that "the German fleet was 400 miles off Montevideo" the previous evening, but no one believed it. The next day we left dinner hurriedly; a signal was received, "Alter course together" to starboard 60 degrees. We altered and stood by for action, but it only turned out to be a British vessel—a false alarm which, however, was excellent practice. Information came through on the 3rd that the German tender *Patagonia* left Montevideo during the night with stores for the German warships; therefore presumably they were not far off.

We arrived off Port Stanley on the morning of December 7th, and were piloted into harbour through a channel in the line of mines, which had been hastily constructed from empty oil-drums, and laid across the entrance by the *Canopus*. As there were only three colliers here, the ships were ordered to coal in turn; the remainder, under convoy of the *Orama*, were following us down from the base.

The Falkland Islands number about two hundred only two of which, East and West Falkland, are of any size. The coast line of both these islands is deeply indented and much resembles one of the Outer Hebrides. Devoid of all trees, the dark brown and green moors, relieved here and there by patches of granite quartz, look uninviting, but abound in penguins hares, and sheep. Some of us, being unable to coal ship, landed on the day of our arrival and shot some hares and geese—a welcome change for the larder. It was the breeding season, and the penguin camps or rookeries were a striking sight; on approaching them hundreds would stand up and waddle forward in a threatening attitude, making a terrible din in order to protect their eggs. So numerous are they compared with the inhabitants that the Governor is locally called the "King of the Penguins."

The little town of Port Stanley, the capital, lies on the south side of the inner portion of a harbour on the east coast of East Falkland, and consists of two streets of houses, almost all, except Government House and the cathedral, constructed of timber and corrugated iron. It is very much like one of the new small towns of Canada. The principal fuel is peat, which may be seen stacked as in Ireland. The population numbers about a thousand, and another thousand—mostly farmers and shepherds of Scottish origin— live out on the moors of the islands.

During the summer the temperature averages about 48° Fahr., and it is nearly always blowing hard, raining, hailing, or snowing. Situated in a cold current from the Antarctic, the temperature only falls eleven degrees in the winter; as a result, scarcely any of the inhabitants can swim, it being too cold to bathe. Owing to the absence of sun and summer heat, wheat, oats, and English vegetables do not thrive, but the colony is none the less remarkably healthy.

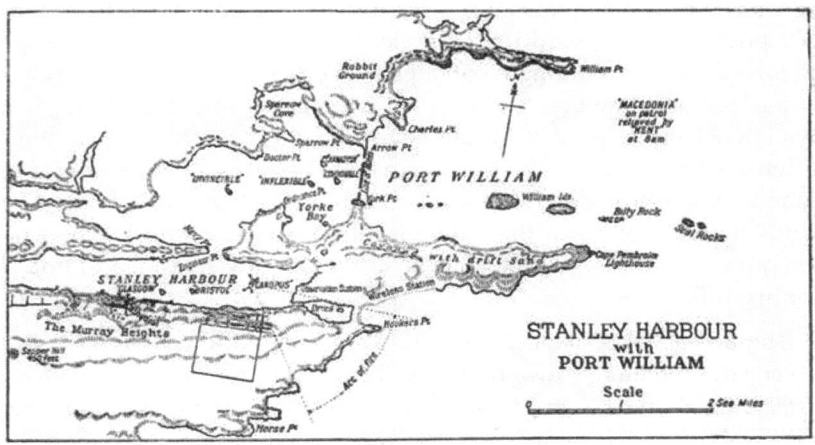

STANLEY HARBOUR with PORT WILLIAM

When the news of the Coronel disaster reached them, the islanders were naturally much concerned for their safety. They had a volunteer corps of a few hundred men, which took to training most assiduously and quickly improved in efficiency. Every man was a good horseman and proficient with the rifle, but the corps were not sufficiently numerous to prevent a landing. A council of war was held by the Governor, at which the position was fully discussed. It seemed only too probable that the Germans would attack the Islands, and arrangements were made to send away from Stanley the few women and children. Stores of provisions were secreted within easy reach of the town, and the public money, official documents, confidential books, and valuables were either removed to a place of safety or buried.

This was the position when the *Canopus* and the *Glasgow* arrived on November 8th. Sailing the same evening, the *Canopus*, when half-way to Montevideo, was ordered by the Admiralty to return and guard the colony.

On November 13th a warship was sighted from the signal station at Port Stanley making straight towards the harbour from the eastward, an unusual direction from which to approach. The volunteers were called out by the church bells sounding the alarm, and every preparation was made to resist a landing; the *Canopus* on her part could get no reply from the wireless station, so was only able to conclude that Port Stanley had fallen into the enemy's hands. When it was seen that the visitor was none other than the *Canopus*, the feelings of joy and relief were universal and knew no bounds.

Most of the inhabitants buried all their worldly goods of any value, some using their back gardens, which are lightly fenced off from one another, whilst others even carried furniture some distance inland. Several amusing stories resulted. One of these Scots, from the window of his house, had watched his neighbour burying a tin box, and had carefully noted its exact position. Being hard up, he scaled the fence that night and dug up and forced the box. Finding it contained sovereigns, he helped himself to a portion, replaced the box, and covered it over carefully with earth. A few days later, temptation getting the better of him, he paid his neighbour's garden another visit; on the third occasion, however, he was caught red-handed. When brought to book his defence was that as they were such friends he had not taken the whole lot the first time, which would have been quite easy to do, but only a little just when it was needed to tide him over his difficulties.

The *Bristol*, *Glasgow*, and *Inflexible* were ordered to coal as soon as we arrived, the remainder awaiting their turn. The *Carnarvon*, *Cornwall*, and *Bristol* were allowed to put fires out to clean boilers and make adjustments to the valves and machinery of the main engines, in preparation for a protracted sea voyage. The *Macedonia* patrolled the entrance to the harbour, the *Kent* being ordered to relieve her at 8 o'clock the following morning. The *Bristol* and *Glasgow*, being of light draught, proceeded into the inner harbour, but the rest of the squadron anchored in the outer harbour, Port William, as will be seen from the plan.

There is no telegraph cable to the Falklands, so that it was obvious the first point of attack by the enemy would be the wireless station. To protect this the *Canopus* entered the inner harbour, forced herself aground on the muddy bottom, and moored taut head and stern in a position that would enable her to command the southern approach. Here she was able to fire over the narrow neck of low-lying land, that at the same time served partially to conceal her. An observation station, connected with the ship by telephone, was set up ashore, with an elaborate plan for obtaining the bearing and elevation for the guns. Top-masts were housed, and the ship, masts, and funnels were painted all the colours of the rainbow in great big splodges to render her less visible. A look-out station was set up in Sparrow Cove, and three 12-pounder batteries were hastily constructed to dominate the approaches. The landing and placing of these guns, together with the digging of the emplacements, called for a great deal of hard work. Every credit is due to the *Canopus* for the admirable manner in which she dealt with the situation.

Major Turner, who was in command of the Falkland Island Volunteers, was indefatigable in his efforts to prepare efficient land defences. This corps gave valuable assistance to the *Canopus*, co-operating in the work of preparing the coast defences. Prior to the arrival of the *Canopus*, their only guns were a 12-pounder 8-cwt. field gun which had been lent by the *Glasgow*, and a few very antique muzzle-loading field guns.

CHAPTER X
ENEMY IN SIGHT

"And from the crow's nest of the Golden Hynde
A seaman cried, 'By God, the hunt is up!'"
—Alfred Noyes (*Drake*).

December 8th, 1914, was apparently to prove an exception to the general rule in the Falklands, where it usually rains for twenty-one days during the last month of the year, for a perfect mid-summer's morning gave every promise of a fine day to follow. The prospect of a busy day coaling, and taking in stores, brought with it thoughts of the morrow when we were to set forth on our quest after the enemy. The colliers went their round from ship to ship, and the rattling of the winches hoisting the coal inboard never ceased.

At 7.56 A.M. the *Glasgow* fired a gun to attract the attention of the *Invincible*, who was busy coaling, to the signal of the *Canopus* reporting smoke in sight to the south.

Shortly after 8 A.M. the officers in the *Cornwall* were all sitting at breakfast when the Chief Yeoman of Signals entered with a beaming face, full of news, to report that cruisers were in sight to the southward. The general opinion was that some Japanese cruisers were probably coming to join us, and attention was again turned to breakfast.

About 8.15 A.M. came a signal from the flag ship: "Raise steam for full speed, report when ready." Rumour had been so rife of late that we still remained sceptical until a few minutes later news came from the signal station on Sapper Hill that two hostile men-of-war were approaching from the southward, and shortly after that smoke was visible beyond these vessels.

It afterwards transpired that a lady named Mrs. Felton, the wife of a sheep farmer living near Point Pleasant, in the south of the Island, sent her maid and house-boy to the top of a ridge to report everything they saw whilst she telephoned the sighting of the enemy's ships to the nearest signal station, from which it was passed to Port Stanley. She continued to send messages reporting every subsequent movement of the German ships. The three German colliers, two of which were sunk, were also first sighted by her and duly reported. She afterwards received a silver salver from the Admiralty in recognition of her prompt action, and her maid a silver teapot, whilst the signalman at Sapper Hill, Port Stanley, received £5 from Admiral Sturdee—a fact we had cause to remember later on, when frequent reports of "hearing distant firing," "sighting smoke," resulted in one or two wild-goose chases!

"Enemy in sight." What a thrilling message for us all! We could scarcely believe our ears. "What a stroke of luck!" was the general comment. But this was no time for ruminating; deeds, not words, were required. At last "the Day" for which we had prepared had dawned. In very truth the hunt was up. The magic news travelled round the ship's company like lightning, and they fell in in record time—in spite of having to forgo some of their breakfast. The *Invincible, Inflexible,* and *Carnarvon* were in the middle of coaling. Colliers were cast off, and all ships prepared for action in case the enemy appeared off the entrance to Port William.

As several of our ships had one engine down at six hours' notice, the bustle and activity in the engine rooms may well be imagined. We on deck naturally enough were soon ready, and chafed at the delay.

The *Kent* went out of harbour to reconnoitre, to report on the movements of the enemy, and to relieve the *Macedonia*. The enemy's two leading ships—the *Gneisenau* and *Nürnberg*—were in sight and were approaching the wireless station, intending to wreck it. When near the Wolf Rocks they stopped engines and turned to the north-eastward. The bearing and elevation of the enemy ships having been telephoned from the observation station, the *Canopus*, finding that they could get no closer, opened fire over the low neck of land at 9.20 A.M. with her 12-inch guns, firing five rounds at a range of 12,000 yards. It was the first time that most of us had heard a shot fired in a naval action, and it brought home very forcibly the fact that we should soon be tackling the job to which we had looked forward for so long. Hoisting their colours, the enemy turned away S.E. to join the main squadron, which headed out to the eastward. It afterwards transpired that the Germans had seen the tripod masts of our battle-cruisers over the land, which probably decided von Spee in turning away from his objective. In one moment all his hopes of destroying our Fleet—supposed to consist of *Carnarvon, Cornwall* and *Bristol,* and possibly the *Canopus* and *Glasgow*—the wireless station, and then capturing the colony, were dashed to the ground. From survivors it appears that one of the *Canopus's* shells had ricocheted, striking the *Gneisenau* at the base of her after funnel; it was also claimed that a piece of another hit the *Nürnberg*—good shooting by indirect fire at such a range, with guns of an old type and improvised fire-control arrangements.

Officers of the *Canopus*, who were in the observation station ashore, saw through the telescope of their theodolite the men on board the *Gneisenau* fallen in on deck; they could be distinguished, quite plainly, dressed ready for landing, in order to capture the wireless station under cover of their ship's guns. But when the *Canopus* opened fire with her first two projectiles they lost no time in scuttling away to their action stations.

An amusing incident occurred on board the *Canopus* when the enemy first hove in sight. The stokers off watch climbed up inside the foremost funnel to see what was going on and sat round the edge, feeling quite secure as they knew the ship was ashore—hard and fast. They very soon came down, however, when they were informed that the boilers of that funnel were being lit up and the ship going to sea.

At 9.40 A.M. the *Glasgow* went out to join the *Kent* in observing the enemy's movements. Five minutes later the squadron weighed, with the exception of the *Bristol*, who had all her fires out to clean boilers. She was ready three-quarters of an hour later, however, which must have constituted a record for ships of her class. The *Carnarvon*, *Inflexible*, *Invincible*, and *Cornwall* proceeded out in the order named, the *Inflexible* ramming a sailing pinnace belonging to the *Cornwall*, half full of stores, on her way through the line of mines; fortunately a barrel of beer belonging to the wardroom officers had previously been rescued! The *Macedonia* was ordered to remain behind in Port William. It was very clear with a slight north-westerly breeze—ideal conditions for a long-range action.

The last of our line cleared the harbour about 10.30 A.M., when the five enemy ships could be seen hull down on the horizon to the S.E., 12 to 13 miles off, steaming off in the hopeless attempt to escape. The signal "General chase" was flying from the *Invincible*, and the magnificent spectacle of our ships, each with four or five white ensigns fluttering in the breeze, all working up to full speed, will always live in the memory of those who witnessed it on that eventful day.

The surprise and horror of the Germans at seeing our two battle-cruisers for the first time was testified by the survivors, who said, "They tried not to believe it." It must have been an awful moment finding themselves suddenly face to face with almost certain destruction. First of our ships came the little *Glasgow*, dashing along like an express train, then the two huge battle-cruisers going about 25 knots, belching forth volumes of dense black smoke as they made use of their oil fuel to quicken their fires, followed by the *Kent*, *Carnarvon*, and *Cornwall* doing about 22 knots.

The Admiral reduced speed for an hour to 20 knots at 11.15 A.M., to allow the "County" cruisers to catch up, for it was evident that we were rapidly gaining on the enemy, as we sped along on an easterly course. The *Glasgow* was ordered to keep three miles ahead of the *Invincible*. There was now an opportunity to get out of coaling kit and have a hasty wash. The ship's companies were consequently sent to dinner early, acting on the good old maxim that a man always fights better on a full stomach; but the excitement was too intense for most men to have more than a bite, and they were mostly to be seen crowding about the ship's decks munching a hastily made sandwich.

At 11.27 A.M. the *Bristol* reported that the smoke of three steamers, enemy transports, had been sighted from the signal station at Point Pleasant to the southward of the Island, whereupon the Commander-in-Chief ordered the *Bristol* and *Macedonia* to destroy them. They arrived to find only two, both big colliers, the *Baden* and *Santa Isabel*; the *Bristol* took off the crews and then sank the vessels. Half an hour later the *Bristol* learnt the news of the result of the action, and that the sacrifice of their valuable cargoes had been unnecessary. The *Macedonia*, who was first upon the scene, sighted smoke on the horizon, but could see no ship. Rumour had it that this third ship was the *Seydlitz*, and that she had a landing party of armed men and field guns on board, but this has never been substantiated in any way.

The *Glasgow* was ordered back, and at 12.20 P.M. the Commander-in-Chief decided to attack the enemy with the battle-cruisers, whose speed was increased to 25 knots. The enemy were steaming in two divisions in quarter-line, first the *Gneisenau* and *Nürnberg* on the left of the line, then the *Scharnhorst* (flag), *Dresden*, and *Leipzig*; the latter being astern of the remainder of their ships, who were on the starboard bow of our squadron, became the first target. "Action" was sounded, and at once not a soul was to be seen about the decks, each man being busy at his appointed station. The Admiral hoisted the signal "Open fire" at 12.47, and eight minutes later the *Inflexible* fired at the *Leipzig* the first round of the action; the *Invincible* followed almost immediately afterwards. Both ships were now going their full speed, nearly 27 knots, and firing slowly and deliberately at the great range of 16,000 yards (over nine land miles). The huge columns of water, over 150 feet high, thrown up by our 12-inch projectiles, which weigh 840 lb., sometimes completely blotted out the enemy target at this distance. Owing to the German ships being end-on, it was difficult to get the direction, but our shots were falling very close to them at times, and soon produced a drastic change in their movements.

Admiral von Spee is said to have now made this signal to his ships: "The armoured cruisers will engage the enemy *as long as possible*, the light cruisers are to use every endeavour to escape." Acting on this, at 1.20 P.M. the *Dresden*, the *Nürnberg*—which one of our battle-cruisers claimed to have hit—and the *Leipzig* turned away to the southward, the positions of the ships being roughly as shown in the plan The *Scharnhorst* and *Gneisenau* will be seen turning to port to engage the battle-cruisers, which altered simultaneously on to a parallel course, whilst the remainder of our squadron, except the *Carnarvon*, which presumably had orders to proceed with the Commander-in-Chief, turned and gave chase to the *Dresden, Leipzig*, and *Nürnberg*. The *Carnarvon* was, of course, unable to keep up with the big ships, and did not get into action until later; she was now 10 miles astern, and altered course to port to cut a corner and join the Flag.

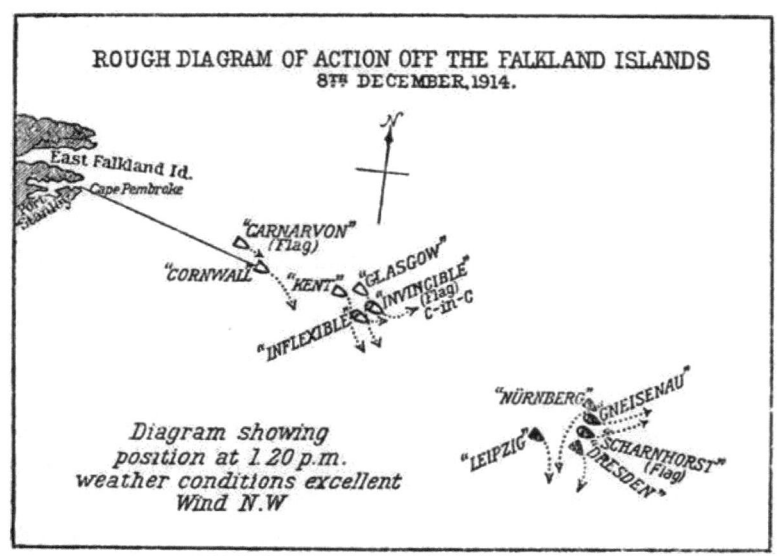

ROUGH DIAGRAM OF ACTION OFF THE
FALKLAND ISLANDS 8TH DECEMBER, 1914.

All this while the "County" cruisers were coming along with all possible speed. The *Glasgow* was stationed clear of the battle-cruisers, which were followed by the *Kent, Cornwall,* and *Carnarvon*. When the action commenced the crews of these ships had the most perfect view of a modern naval engagement fought at long range. As an officer in the *Kent* described it: "We were spectators in the front row of the stalls, as it were, so close that we could almost touch the actors on the stage, yet so far that no stray missile disturbed the comfort of our view. The best seats in the house at a performance of one of the few remaining spectacles which cannot be bought for money."

Imagine a calm, smooth sea, the sun shining and not a cloud in the sky, the ship steaming at something over 23 knots, and the men crowded on the turrets and in every available corner, tier upon tier, for all the world as if looking on at a cup tie at the Crystal Palace.... It was a wonderful sight. The big ships buried their sterns in the sea, throwing up the seething water in their wakes as they dashed onwards. The bright flashes of their guns showed up strikingly, followed successively by the dark brown puffs of cordite smoke; the seconds were counted until the reports were heard and huge columns of water thrown up by the splashes were seen. Many of the men had had friends in the *Good Hope* and *Monmouth* whose fate was fresh in their minds. "Give 'em one for the *Monmouth*!" and "Go on, boys, give 'em hell—let the blighters feel what it's like!" were shouted quite unconsciously, punctuated by loud cheers when a salvo pitched perilously close to the enemy ships. Of course, the majority realised our superiority, but those in authority must have felt a pride in such men who gave the impression they would face odds with intrepidity.

The battle now divided itself into two separate engagements, the battle-cruisers and the *Carnarvon*, which were engaging the two enemy armoured cruisers, and the *Cornwall*, *Kent*, and *Glasgow*, which gave chase to the light cruisers. Later, a third action developed when the *Kent* went after the *Nürnberg*. Each of these will be taken in turn and described separately.

CHAPTER XI
THE BATTLE-CRUISER ACTION

"Are hell-gates burst at last? For the black deep
To windward burns with streaming crimson fires!
Over the wild strange waves, they shudder and creep
Nearer—strange smoke-wreathed masts and spare, red spires
And blazing hulks."

— Alfred Noyes (*Drake*).

A few minutes after the German light-cruisers turned away to the S.S.E. in accordance with his orders, Admiral Count von Spee, apparently deciding to accept the inevitable, determined to try and close so as to get into the effective range of his 8.2-inch guns. With this intention, his two armoured cruisers turned in succession about 80 degrees to port, which brought them into line-ahead with the *Gneisenau* leading, and then opened fire at 1.30 P.M. But he had reckoned without his host, as this very obvious manœuvre did not at all suit Admiral Sturdee's book, who was acting on the principle that ammunition is cheaper than human life, and was resolved to fight at his own chosen range. Our ships, therefore, eased speed to 24 knots, and turned together away from the enemy to port, which brought them at the same time into line-ahead with the flag ship *Invincible* in the van.

The two squadrons were on nearly parallel courses (*see* facing). The *Inflexible* had checked fire for a while, but now reopened on the *Scharnhorst* at a range of 14,500 yards. Both the enemy ships concentrated their fire on the *Invincible* at this time, whilst ours fired each at his opponent. The respective armaments are seen from the following:

Name	Tonnage	Armament	Speed	Completion	Armour Belt
Invincible }	17,250	{ 8—12" }	26	{ 1909	7 to 4 in.
Inflexible }		{ 16—4" }		{ 1908	7 to 4 in.
Carnarvon	10,850	4—7.5"	22	1903	7 to 4 in.
		6—6"			

Scharnhorst }		{ 8—8.2" }	23.5	1908	6 to 3 in.
}	11,420	{ 6—5.9" }			
Gneisenau }		{ 20—3.4" }	23.8	1908	6 to 3 in.

Compiled from "Brassey's Naval Annual."

As Admiral Sturdee edged away and did not allow the range to get below 13,500 yards, the fire of the Germans was not effective. A gunnery officer stated that their fire control was efficient, and that their salvoes, fired frequently, fell well together, the spread being about 200 yards. They had been firing about ten minutes when the *Scharnhorst* went ahead and took the lead, so our ships changed targets. For a short time both German ships now fired at the *Inflexible*, but without result; soon afterwards they again honoured the *Invincible* with their attentions, and, getting the range, scored their first hit about 1.45 P.M. The range was now increased, spotting the fall of shot became more and more difficult, and finally smoke interfered with our gunfire. At 2 P.M. the distance of the enemy was 16,450 yards. Ten minutes later von Spee turned right away and made a second attempt to escape, as he had been unable to get to close quarters. We turned gradually after him, but as he continued to turn away, in the words of Admiral Sturdee, "A second chase ensued." All firing ceased, and there was an appreciable lull in the proceedings.

Of the damage to the *Scharnhorst* at this time no estimate can be formed, but survivors from the *Gneisenau* stated that they had three direct hits, resulting in fifty men being killed and wounded. To the uninitiated this may seem to be poor shooting; but the difficulty of seeing clearly enough to make accurate corrections to the gunsights, the extreme range, and the disturbing effect of the enemy's fire must all be taken into account. Doubtless, too, there were several hits of an insignificant nature on the upper works and rigging that were not taken into account. It was impossible to tell at such a long range whether we scored a hit unless a fire resulted.

The efficiency of the engine-room staff was now put to the test; they nobly responded, with the result that our big ships attained a greater speed than they had ever done before.

At this juncture a full-rigged sailing ship appeared on the port hand of our battle-cruisers; she was painted white, and her sails were shining as if bleached in the bright sunlight; with stunsails and every stitch of canvas spread she sailed majestically along, looking a perfect picture. So close was she that the Admiral was forced to alter his course to pass a couple of miles clear of her, so that the enemy's shell ricocheting should not hit her. Truly it must have been a thrilling and dramatic moment for her to find herself an involuntary witness of such a wonderful spectacle! Imagine her consternation at being plunged suddenly into the middle of a red-hot naval action between powerfully armed modern men-of-war, with shell falling in the water quite close alongside.

The distance of the retreating enemy was rapidly decreasing, until at 2.45 P.M. Admiral Sturdee gave the order to open fire at a range of about 15,000 yards. Von Spee held on his course in the vain hope, apparently, of drawing us on, so that by a sudden turn made later he might "get to grips." Eight minutes afterwards the Germans were forced to turn to port towards us, forming into line-ahead and opening fire as soon as they came round. We hauled out once again on to an almost parallel course. The range had appreciably dropped, and was at one time under 12,000 yards. Things now became fast and furious, shot and bursting shell were everywhere in the air, and our 12-inch guns were doing terrible execution. "It was like hell let loose," said a petty officer in the flagship, which was hit several times. The German gunnery was not nearly as good as it had been in the first phase of the engagement, whilst we had settled down to business and were, on the whole, more accurate than before. An officer in the *Inflexible* remarked that at this time several of the enemy's shell fell between our two ships and that as his ship approached these yellow-green patches, he wondered whether the debatable maxim that no two projectiles ever hit the same spot would prove accurate.

The *Scharnhorst* was badly hit at 3 P.M., starting a fire forward, but she continued to blaze away; the *Gneisenau* also bore signs of the severe treatment she had received from the *Inflexible*. The *Invincible* now met with some damage, and suffered by far the most as the enemy's fire was naturally concentrated on her. The wind had increased, and was blowing the smoke across the guns, impeding our gunners, and the *Carnarvon* was coming up astern, so at 3.18 Admiral Sturdee executed a sudden manœuvre by putting his helm over to starboard, turning completely around, and crossing his own track so as to steer roughly S.W.; this put the enemy completely off the range, and also forced him five minutes later on to a parallel course, in order to avoid the alternative of being raked fore and aft. As both our ships had altered course together, their respective positions became reversed— the *Inflexible* leading—and they presented their port sides to the enemy (*see* facing). The *Carnarvon* cut the corner and came up on the off side of the battle-cruisers, in accordance with Admiral Sturdee's orders, as her guns were useless at ranges exceeding 12,000 yards. The *Scharnhorst*, who had already had a bad hammering from the flagship, was now subjected to the concentrated fire of our two big ships for a very short time, during which the *Gneisenau* was lost sight of in her consort's smoke. At 3.30 P.M. the

Scharnhorst's fire had slackened perceptibly, and one shell had shot away her third funnel.

The *Invincible* now engaged the *Gneisenau*, who was not nearly so badly damaged and was firing all her guns. In fact, all ships were at it as hard as they could go, but the *Inflexible* came off lightly on account of the plight of her opponent. The noise was indescribable, shell were hurtling through the rigging; when one actually struck and burst, the whole ship quivered and staggered, while the crash of steel plates falling, and splinters of shell striking the upper works, sounded like hundreds of empty tins being hurled against one another.

The *Scharnhorst* was clearly in a very bad way, and looked, as she was, a perfect wreck. Masses of steel were twisted and torn as if growing out in all directions like the roots of a tree, clouds of steam were going up sky high, and she was blazing fore and aft. The Admiral says, "At times a shell would cause a large hole to appear in her side, through which could be seen a dull red glow of flame." She was 14,000 yards distant. Up till quite near the end, however, she continued to fire in salvos, her starboard guns having only been in action since the last turn was made. At 3.56 P.M. the Commander-in-Chief decided to close in and give her the *coup de grace*, which enabled the Carnarvon to get into action and open fire for the first time. By 4 P.M. both the *Scharnhorst's* masts, as well as her three funnels, were shot away, and she was listing heavily to port. She struggled on hopelessly and went over more and more, until at 4.10 P.M. she was on her beam ends. For seven minutes she remained in this position, her screws still going round, and then suddenly sank like a stone, with her flag still flying.

Shortly before the German flagship sank, our ships checked fire and then opened on the *Gneisenau*. It will be seen from the plan of the action that at the time the *Invincible* turned two complete circles in a sort of figure of eight, the *Gneisenau* hesitated for a minute or two as to whether she should stand by her consort to save life. Under the impression, apparently, that our flagship, which had turned towards the *Scharnhorst*, was about to pick up survivors, the *Gneisenau* passed on the far side of the sinking ship and opened a heavy and well-directed fire on the *Inflexible*. We were now three against one, who was, nevertheless, determined to sell herself as dearly as possible. It was a gallant attempt.

The distance was fortunately too great to see clearly the wretched survivors of the *Scharnhorst* left struggling hopelessly against their fate, but it brought the dark side of war very vividly into notice for the first time. A quarter of an hour after she sank the *Carnarvon* passed over the exact spot, but neither survivors nor wreckage were to be seen.

The weather now changed, a light drizzling mist obscuring the former visibility. It was obvious that there could be only one end to the fight now in progress, and that it could not long be delayed. At 4.15 P.M. the *Invincible* opened fire on the *Gneisenau*, which shifted her target from the *Inflexible* and fired at the flagship with creditable precision. She was "straddling" the *Invincible* at 4.25, the range being about 10,000 yards, so this was increased. During the next quarter of an hour our flagship was hit three times, but the German was taking terrible punishment. At 4.47 she ceased firing; her colours had been shot away several times, but she had hoisted them again and again. Now, however, no colours were to be seen, so it was only natural to conclude she had struck, though it was afterwards ascertained that she had no more left to hoist. Our ships turned to avoid getting too far off, when, to the surprise of all, she suddenly fired off a solitary gun, showing that she was still game. Unlike her late consort, which looked a perfect wreck for some time before actually sinking, she had to all appearances suffered very little. At 5.8 P.M., however, her foremost funnel went by the board.

The carnage and destruction wrought in the *Gneisenau* by our three ships were terrible, and it was astonishing what a deal of hammering she was still able to bear. That her casualties at this time were very heavy was beyond doubt, as shell were to be seen tearing up her decks as they burst, while the upper works became a veritable shambles. It was not till 5.15 that the doomed ship, being badly hit between the third and fourth funnels, showed real signs of being *in extremis*. She was still firing, however, and even scored an effective hit—the last one she was to get—about this period.

At 5.30 she was obviously dead beat and turned towards our squadron with a heavy list to starboard, afire fore and aft, and steam issuing in dense clouds from all directions. Admiral Sturdee now ordered "Cease fire," but before the signal could be hoisted *Gneisenau* opened fire again, and continued to keep it up with her one remaining undamaged gun. This was returned until it was silenced, when our ships closed in on her. The ensign flying at her foremast head was hauled down at 5.40, but the one at her peak was left flying. Five minutes later she again fired, but only one solitary round, after which she maintained silence. The signal was made to cease firing immediately afterwards, when it was evident that her gallant struggle was at an end.

She now heeled over quite slowly, giving her men plenty of time to get up on deck. At 6 P.M. our ships were perhaps 4,000 yards off, and the Germans could be seen gathering together on her "forecastle quarter deck." Remaining on her beam ends for a few seconds, during which the men were seen clambering about on her side, she quite gently subsided and disappeared without any explosion, although a film of steamy haze hovered over the spot where she sank. The bow remained poised for a second or two, after which she foundered at 6.2 in latitude 52° 40′ S., longitude 56° 20′ W., having withstood the combined fire of our ships for an hour and forty-five minutes.

The sea was no longer quite calm, and a misty, drizzling rain was falling. Closing in hastily, every effort was made to save life, and boats were got out and lowered. This is no easy job after an action, as the boats are turned inboard, resting on their crutches, and are kept partially filled with water in case a shell might strike them and cause a fire. This water must first be drained out, then the weight of the boat is hoisted on to the slips to enable it to be swung outboard, which is not easy if the ship has been hit near the water-line, causing a list. Finally, several of the boats are certain to be riddled with shell splinters.

A midshipman, describing the scene that followed, writes, "We cast overboard every rope's end we can and try our hands at casting to some poor wretch feebly struggling within a few yards of the ship's side. Missed him! Another shot. He's further off now! Ah! the rope isn't long enough. No good; try someone else. He's sunk now!"

The men, however, had not yet heard of the rough weather during the Coronel action, and still thought that the Germans might have saved our poor fellows there. Lines were thrown over with shouts of, "Here, Sausage, put this round your belly," and the like. Taking into consideration that it was estimated some 600 men had been killed or wounded, and that the temperature of the water was 40°, it was fortunate that as many as 170 officers and men were rescued. The gallant Admiral Count von Spee, whose conduct bears out the best traditions of naval history, and his two sons, all lost their lives in the course of the day.

A curious feature of this action was the terrific damage done by 12-inch lyddite shell. One of the *Gneisenau's* turrets was severed from its trunk and blown bodily overboard. Nearly every projectile that hit caused a fire, which was often promptly extinguished by the splash of the next one falling short. Indeed, it was stated by the prisoners that the guns' crews in the German ships were frequently working their guns up to their knees in water, and towards the latter part of the engagements were unable to fire on account of the volume of water thrown up by short shots.

The *Invincible* had been hit about twenty-two times, but the fighting efficiency of the ship was not affected. Eighteen of these were direct hits, two being below the water-line on the port side, one of which flooded a bunker and gave her a list to port. There were no casualties, however, amongst her complement of 950. The *Inflexible* was only hit directly twice; she had one man killed and three slightly wounded. Her main derrick was cut in two, so that she was unable to use her steam boats. The few casualties speak more eloquently than any words of the tactics adopted by Admiral Sturdee in putting to the greatest possible use the heavier armament at his disposal.

The *Invincible* had some interesting damage. One 8.2-inch shell burst and completely wrecked her wardroom, making a gigantic hole in her side. Two others hit the stalk of her after conning tower and burst, but did no damage to the inmates, who only complained of the fumes being sweet and sickly, leaving an unpleasant taste which, however, soon wore off. Another interesting case was the extraordinary damage done by a spent projectile falling at an angle of fifty degrees. Passing close under her forebridge, it cut the muzzle of one of her 4-inch guns clean off, after which it passed through the steel deck, through a ventilating trunk, through the deck below, and finished up in the Admiral's storeroom—side by side with the cheese, which put the finishing touch to its career. Another shell caused a nasty hole on the water-line, seven feet by three, which was found to be beyond the capabilities of the ship's staff to repair temporarily. The bunker had to be left flooded, all the surrounding bulkheads being carefully shored up and strengthened until she returned to England. In "A Naval Digression"[8] "G. F." says: "On a part of the main deck one might have imagined for a second that a philanthropist had been at work, for there, strewn about, were a thousand odd golden sovereigns; a shell had come through the upper deck, and, visiting the Fleet-Paymaster's cabin, had 'upset' the money chest. It had then gone through the bulkhead into the chaplain's cabin next door, and finally passed out through the ship's side, taking with it a large part of the reverend gentleman's wardrobe, and reducing to rags and tatters most of what it had the decency to leave behind."

The Commander of the *Gneisenau* was picked up by the *Inflexible*, and gave some interesting details. Describing the time when the *Canopus* fired at the *Gneisenau* and *Nürnberg* on their first approach to Port Stanley, he told us that he said to his Captain, "Captain, we must either fight or go faster," adding that in his opinion the day would have ended very differently had they come up boldly off the mouth of the harbour and bombarded our ships at anchor before they were able to get out. There can be no doubt that the issue would have been the same, but the Germans might have been able to inflict some serious damage, especially to those ships lying nearest the mouth of the harbour, who would have masked the battle-cruisers' fire. However, his Captain elected to run, so they went "faster."

During the action he had to go round the ship with the fire-master, putting out any fires that were discovered. Whilst going his rounds during the engagement he found a stoker near one of the drinking tanks on the mess deck, who said he had come up to get a drink of water. The Hun Commander told him that he had no business to leave his post, and, drawing his revolver, shot him dead where he stood.

A curious yarn is connected with Admiral Stoddart, who was in the *Carnarvon*. He had a distant cousin in the German Navy whom he had never met and about whose career he had frequently been asked in years gone by. This cousin of his was one of those saved by the *Carnarvon*, and when he got aboard he said, "I believe I have a cousin in one of the British ships. His name is Stoddart." To find he was the Admiral on board that very ship must have indeed given him what the sailor terms "a fair knock out." He stated that practically every man on the upper deck of the *Gneisenau* was either killed or wounded, and that it was a feat of the greatest difficulty to climb across the deck, so great was the havoc wrought in all directions.

Another officer, who was stationed in one of the 8.2-inch turrets, had a remarkable experience. The turret was hit by a 12-inch shell, and he emerged the sole survivor. He then went on to a casemate, which was also knocked out and most of the crew killed. Trying a third gun, he was perhaps even more fortunate, as it was also hit by a 12-inch shell, and the same thing happened, but shortly after the ship sank and he was saved! This hero was a fat, young lieutenant, who apparently drowned his sorrows the evening before he quitted the *Carnarvon*. Before retiring to bed he stood up in the mess, drink in hand, bowed blandly to everyone and said, with a broad smile on his fat face, "Gentlemen, I thank you very much — you have been very kind to me, and I wish you all in Hell!"

The wisdom of Admiral Sturdee's orders to the *Carnarvon* to keep out of range of the Germans was brought home by an officer survivor of the *Gneisenau*, who said that they knew they were done and had orders "to concentrate on the *little* ship and sink her if she came within range!"

Upwards of 600 men had been killed or wounded when the *Gneisenau's* ammunition was finally expended. The German captain "fell-in" the remainder and told them to provide themselves with hammocks or any woodwork they could find, in order to support themselves in the water.

A certain number of the German sailors that were rescued from the icy ocean succumbed to exposure and shock, though the proportion was very small. They were given a naval funeral with full military honours and were buried at sea the day after the battle. When the funeral service was about to take place on the quarter-deck of one of our warships, the German prisoners were told to come aft to attend it. On rounding the superstructure, however, the leading men suddenly halted dead, brought up aghast with fright at the sight of the guard of armed marines falling in across the deck, who were about to pay the last tributes of military honours to the dead. When ordered on, these terrified Huns point blank refused to move, being convinced that the Marine Guard was there in order to shoot them!

CHAPTER XII
THE END OF THE "LEIPZIG"

"War raged in heaven that day ...
... Light against darkness, Liberty
Against all dark old despotism, unsheathed
The sword in that great hour."

— Alfred Noyes (*Drake*).

It will be recollected that during the chase the battle-cruisers were firing at the *Leipzig* before the main battle with Admiral von Spee took place. This compelled the Germans to divide into two separate squadrons, since a direct hit from a 12-inch gun might easily prove fatal to one of their light-cruisers. Foreseeing that this manœuvre was likely to occur, Admiral Sturdee had directed the *Cornwall, Kent,* and *Glasgow* to follow in pursuit. No time was lost, therefore, in giving chase to the enemy light-cruisers when they turned off to the S.S.E. at 1.20 P.M., the *Glasgow* leading the way at 26 knots, followed by the *Kent* and the *Cornwall* keeping neck and neck and going about 23½ knots. The *Dresden* led the enemy light-cruisers with the *Leipzig* and *Nürnberg* on her starboard and port quarter respectively.

In the ever-increasing distance between our two squadrons, the main battle could still be seen through field glasses, which made the necessity for turning away from a spectacle of such absorbing and compelling interest all the more tantalising. But there was solid work to be done, requiring concentration, thought, and cool judgment.

A stern chase is proverbially a long one, and the difference in speed between our ships and the Germans' was not sufficient to justify any hope of getting to business for at least two hours, as the slowest enemy ship was probably doing 23 knots at this time. Every effort was now made to go as fast as possible, and the *Cornwall* and *Kent* had quite an exciting race as they worked up to 24 knots or slightly more—a speed actually exceeding that realised along the measured mile when these ships were new. The engine-room staffs on both ships "dug out for all they were worth," and the keenest rivalry prevailed.

It was very evident that a long chase lay before us, for the *Glasgow* was the only ship of the three that had a marked superiority in speed to the enemy. The *Cornwall* and *Kent* were gaining very slowly but surely on the *Leipzig* and *Nürnberg*, but were losing on the *Dresden*.

The enemy kept edging away to port continually, and about 2.15 we passed over the spot where later in the day the *Gneisenau* was sunk by our battle-cruisers.

About 2.45 P.M. the positions of the ships were as plan. The *Leipzig* was the centre rearmost ship, with the *Dresden* some four to five miles on her starboard bow, while the *Nürnberg* was about a mile on her port bow. Both these ships were diverging slightly from the *Leipzig*, spreading out in the shape of a fan to escape being brought to action. The *Cornwall* and *Kent* were some eleven miles astern of the *Leipzig*, and the *Glasgow* was four miles distant on the starboard bow.

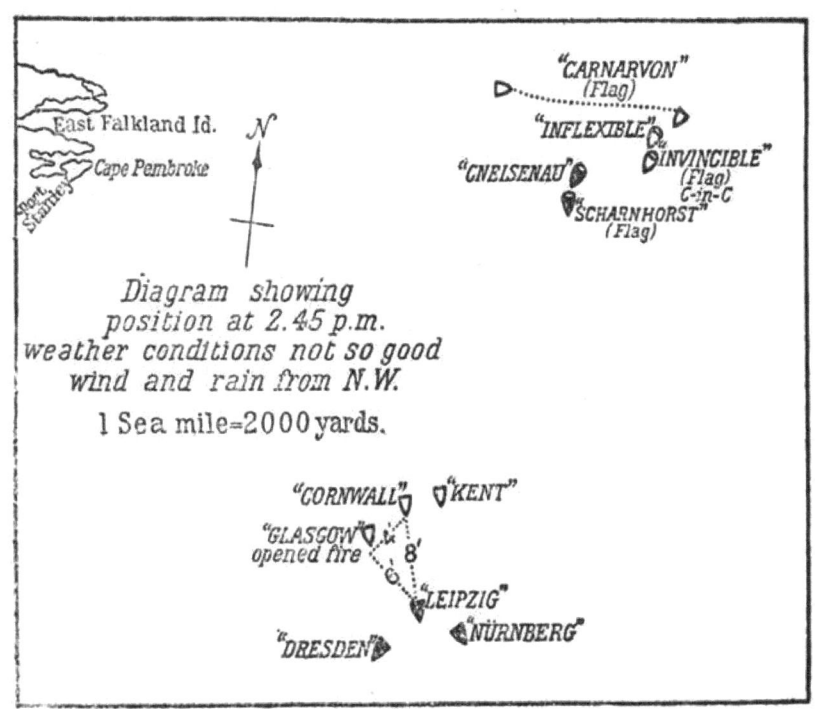

Diagram showing position at 2.45 p.m.
weather conditions not so good wind and rain from N.W.

As the *Glasgow* drew ahead she edged over to starboard in the direction of the *Dresden*. About 3 P.M. she opened fire with her two 6-inch guns on the *Leipzig* at 12,000 yards, in the hope of outranging her and reducing her speed, so that the *Cornwall* and *Kent* might come into action. The *Leipzig*, however, held on her course, and replied to the *Glasgow's* fire, though it was evident that she was at the limit of her gun range. The firing was spasmodic and not very effective.

The *Glasgow's* speed was so much superior to that of the enemy that she soon closed the range very appreciably, and the *Leipzig* was seen to straddle her with her salvoes on more than one occasion. The *Glasgow* therefore altered course outwards, at the same time firing her after 6-inch gun, and then, having opened the range, turned up on to a roughly parallel course with the German. The duel between these ships continued intermittently.

The *Cornwall* and *Kent* were still keeping fairly level, and had closed in to a distance of about half a mile from one another. The chase continued, each minute seeming an age, as the range-finders registered the slowly diminishing distance of the enemy. The crews watched the proceedings from the forecastles with the greatest interest; now and again a half-smothered cheer would break out when the *Glasgow's* shots fell perilously near the mark. When the bugle sounded "Action," the men responded with a spontaneous cheer as they rushed off at the double to their appointed stations. Their spirit was fine.

Captain J. Luce, of the *Glasgow*, was the senior naval officer of our three ships, and at 3.20 P.M. signalled the *Cornwall* to ask, "Are you gaining on the enemy?" To which a reply was made, "Yes—range now 16,000 yards." A quarter of an hour later the *Glasgow* ceased fire for a while. Captain W. M. Ellerton, of the *Cornwall*, now made a signal to the *Kent*: "I will take the centre target (*Leipzig*) if you will take the left-hand one (*Nürnberg*), as we appear to be gaining on both of them." The *Glasgow* again opened fire on the *Leipzig* at 3.45, but her shots falling short, she very soon afterwards ceased fire. At 4.6 the *Glasgow* and *Leipzig* again fired at one another, and shortly afterwards the former was hit twice; an unlucky shot, descending at a steep angle, killed one man and wounded four others.

Captain Luce now found himself face to face with a difficult decision, which had to be made promptly. Was he to use his superior speed and endeavour to cut off the *Dresden* or not? He decided to assist the *Cornwall* and *Kent* in order to make sure of the destruction of the *Leipzig* and *Nürnberg*. At 4.25 P.M. the *Glasgow* turned to starboard away from the action and took station on the port quarter of the *Cornwall*, who had by that time come into action with the *Leipzig*.

During this period the *Cornwall* and *Kent* had been gaining fairly rapidly on the *Leipzig* and slowly on the *Nürnberg*, though losing on the *Dresden*, who was easily the fastest of the three German light-cruisers. The latter kept edging away gradually to starboard, outdistancing her pursuers, and finally made good her escape without firing a single shot.

At a quarter past four the *Cornwall* and the *Kent* opened fire on the *Leipzig* almost simultaneously at a range of 10,900 yards. The effect of this was that the German altered course slightly to starboard and was followed by the *Cornwall*, while the *Kent* went after the *Nürnberg*, as had been arranged.

The *Leipzig* now directed her fire on to the *Cornwall*. At the outset we were astounded to find that her projectiles were falling over us at this distance, but she soon found this out, and most of her splashes were well short for some minutes. As the range diminished the firing became more accurate, and it was possible to judge of its effect. It was not till 4.22 that the *Cornwall* scored her first visible hit, which carried away the enemy's fore-topmast, killing the gunnery lieutenant and disabling the fire control. The enemy thereupon altered course away slightly to starboard, at which we made a bigger turn in the same direction, so as to cut him off, as well as to cross his course the more rapidly in the event of his dropping mines overboard. This manœuvre brought the range down to 8,275 yards at 4.56, when he scored some hits. Captain Ellerton then turned away to starboard to give the enemy a broadside, at the same time opening the range, which completely upset the accuracy of the *Leipzig's* fire.

The *Glasgow* took up her self-appointed station on the port quarter of the *Cornwall* (see Plan), and the action developed into a running fight between our two ships and the *Leipzig*, who concentrated her fire on the *Cornwall*, which, however, had superior armament:

Name	Tonnage	Armament	Speed	Completion
Cornwall	9,800	14—6"	23.68	1904
Glasgow	4,800	2—6"		
		10—4"	25.8	1900
Leipzig	3,200	10—4.1"	23.5	1906

From "Brassey's Naval Annual."

Mist and a light drizzling rain now set in, so we broke into independent firing on account of the difficulty of spotting the fall of shot. The range opened to 9,800 yards, and still we were being hit, which clearly showed the efficiency of the German 4.1-inch gun. Our course soon took us out of range, so we again turned towards the enemy, ceasing fire from 5.12 to 5.29 P.M. This was analogous to the interval that occurred in the battle-cruisers' action, and is significant; both took place on the same day, and both were due to the same cause—namely, the idea of making full use of the heavier armament in our ships, and thus eliminating the risk of incurring unnecessary casualties.

Shortly after 5.30 P.M. the *Cornwall* was hit no fewer than nine times in as many minutes at a range of over 9,000 yards, so course was again altered to starboard, a broadside being fired as the ship turned. We continued these tactics, closing in and firing the foremost group of guns and then turning out again as soon as we had got in too close, at the same time getting in broadside fire, by which we managed to score a number of hits with common shell.

Fire was checked at 5.46, slow salvoes being resorted to on account of the difficulties of spotting. At this time a heavy thud was felt forward, which made the whole ship quiver; a shell had landed in the paint room, where it burst and made rather a mess of things. No material damage resulted, and there was fortunately no fire. At 6.15 we started using lyddite instead of common shell, having again decreased the range. The result was stupendous, the dark smoke and flash caused by those projectiles as they struck could be plainly seen, and not long afterwards the enemy was on fire. His return fire began to slacken appreciably, though he still managed to get a hit every now and again. Captain Ellerton decided to close and went in to nearly 7,000 yards, turning and letting the German have it from the port broadside.

It was now 6.35, and the news came through by wireless from the flagship that the *Scharnhorst* and *Gneisenau* had been sunk. It passed round the ship like lightning, even penetrating the watertight bulkheads in some miraculous manner, and cheered up all hands tremendously.

Keeping the range between 7,000 and 8,000 yards, our ships continued to do great damage, and at 6.51 the enemy was seen to be badly on fire forward. In spite of this he continued to fire with great spirit, and even registered a few hits between 6.55 and 7.45 P.M. Then his firing stopped completely, and it was observed that he was on fire the whole length of the ship. The scuttles showed up like a series of blood-red dots gleaming from the ship's side, the whole of the foremost funnel and part of the centre one had disappeared, the upper works were severely damaged, while smoke was issuing here and there. The ship, indeed, presented a sorry spectacle.

All this time the *Glasgow*, which was still on the quarter of the *Cornwall*, had also been busily engaged with the *Leipzig*, but at a greater range.

We ceased firing at 7.10, thinking that the enemy would strike his colours; but not a bit of it, so three minutes later we reopened fire with reluctance, though only for a couple of minutes. We closed in to 4,700 yards, turning 16 points in order to keep well out of torpedo range, and gave him a few more salvoes of lyddite with our starboard guns. The light was beginning to wane, and though twilight is very prolonged in these southern regions during the summer, it would soon have been too dark to see through the telescopic sights. At 7.43 an explosion took place on board the *Leipzig*; three minutes later the mainmast went slowly over, and finally collapsed with a crash. We waited to give her an opportunity to haul down her colours and surrender, and then opened fire again just before 8 P.M. At last, at 8.12, the Germans sent up two green lights as signals of distress, at which we both immediately closed in, stopped, and proceeded to get out boats. Darkness fell rapidly, and searchlights were turned on to the enemy, lighting up the ghastly scene where men could be seen jumping clear of the ship into the icy-cold water. The *Leipzig* was heeled over to port, almost on her beam ends; she only had a bit of one funnel left, and all the after part of the ship was in flames. The fire on her forecastle had also burst into flame. Thick clouds of white steam escaping, showed up against the dense black smoke, and increased the dramatic effect. Our little boats became visible in the beams of the searchlights, as they rowed round to pick up survivors. At 9.21 P.M. a shower of sparks suddenly announced an explosion, directly after which the *Leipzig* foundered. Several of our boats were holed, and we only succeeded in saving six officers and nine men between the two of us, all of whom, however, survived the extreme cold. They told us that before the ship was abandoned the Kingston valves had been opened.

No further casualties had occurred on board the *Glasgow* since those already mentioned, as after joining the *Cornwall* she had not come under direct fire, although some projectiles intended for the latter did hit her. The *Cornwall* was even more fortunate in having no casualties at all except for a solitary pet canary, in spite of having eighteen direct hits not counting splinter holes, of which there were forty-two in one funnel alone. This absence of casualties, which was also a feature of the battle-cruiser action, speaks for the efficient handling of the ship by Captain Ellerton.

Survivors stated that von Spee was originally going direct to the Plate to coal, but that having captured a sailing vessel full of coal at Cape Horn, he changed his plans and decided to attack the Falkland Islands. It was also stated that the *Leipzig* had a large amount of gold on board.

One of the survivors rescued by the *Cornwall* was a naval reservist, who in time of peace had occupied the post of German interpreter to the Law Courts at Sydney, in Australia. When hauled into the boat the first words he used as soon as he had recovered his breath were: "It's bloody cold" in a perfect English accent. It is a well-known fact that sailors rarely make use of bad language, and the bowman who had hauled him out of the water is said to have fainted! Evidently the language of the Law leaves much to be desired.

The torpedo lieutenant of the *Leipzig* was amongst those saved by the *Cornwall*. When brought alongside he was too exhausted to clamber up the ship's side unaided, but when he reached the upper deck he pulled himself together and stood to attention, saluting our officers at the gangway. When he came into the wardroom later on he explained that he had been on board before as a guest at dinner at the time that the ship paid a visit to Kiel for the regatta in 1909, adding that he little expected then that his next visit would take place under such tragic circumstances.

This officer surprised us all by suddenly asking when the *Cornwall* had had bigger guns put into her, and went on to say that when we fired our "big guns"—meaning when we started to use lyddite shell—the damage was appalling, arms and legs were to be seen all along the decks, and each shell that burst started a fire. He went on to say that the *Cornwall's* firing was very effective and accurate, but doubtless most of the prisoners told their captors the same thing. We explained that the armament had not been changed since the ship was originally built. He also told us that the German captain had assembled all the ship's company when their 1,800 rounds of ammunition were expended, and said, "There is the ensign, and any man who wishes may go and haul it down, but I will not do so." Not a soul moved to carry out the suggestion, but about fifty men, having obtained permission, jumped overboard and must have perished from the cold. There were only eighteen left alive on board at the end, so far as he could judge, and of these sixteen were saved. All the officers carried whistles, which accounted for their being located in the water so easily.

The prisoners naturally wished to glorify themselves, their captain, and their shipmates in the eyes of their fellow-countrymen, before whom they knew that these stories would eventually be repeated. Therefore these yarns about the ensign, the men jumping overboard, and the opening of the Kingston valves must be taken with a grain of salt.

The *Cornwall* had one or two interesting examples of the damage done to a ship by modern high-explosive shell. The most serious was a shell that must have exploded on the water-line, as the ship was rolling, for the side was afterwards found to be indented 5 inches at a position 5 to 6 feet below the water-line, and consequently below the armoured belt, a cross bulkhead being at the precise point of impact. Curious as it may appear, even the paint was untouched, and there was no sign of a direct hit from outboard, except for the bulge that remained and the starting of a good many rivets from their sockets. The cross bulkhead behind was buckled up like corrugated iron, and the two coal bunkers, which had been empty, were flooded, giving the ship a heavy list. When we got into Port William we managed to heel the ship sufficiently to enable our carpenters to get at the leak, and they succeeded in completely stopping it in two days, working day and night—a fine performance, for which Mr. Egford, the carpenter, received the D.S.C., whilst his staff were personally congratulated by the Commander-in-Chief.

Another shell passed through the steel depression rail of the after 6-inch turret, by which it was deflected through the deck at the junction of two cabin bulkheads; it next penetrated the deck below and finally burst on the ship's side, causing a large hole. An amusing incident was connected with this. The projectile cut a fire-hose in half, the business end of which was carried down the hole into one of the officer's cabins, where it continued to pump in water for the remainder of the action. At the end of the day this officer found all his belongings, including his full dress and cocked hat, floating about in two or three feet of water.

Another officer was seated on a box in the ammunition passage waiting for the wounded, when a shell struck the ship's side close by him, the concussion knocking him off. Getting up, he saw the doctor near by, and thought he had kicked him, so asked him angrily what the blazes he thought he was doing. It was not until after a long and heated argument that he could be persuaded to believe that he had not been the victim of a practical joke.

In another case a shell shot away the fire main immediately above one of the stokeholds, which was flooded. Stoker Petty Officer W. A. Townsend and Stoker John Smith were afterwards both decorated with the D.S.M. for "keeping the boiler fires going under very trying circumstances."

It was mentioned before that some ships had leave to open up their machinery for repairs. The *Cornwall* was to have steam at six hours' notice, and had the low-pressure cylinder of the port engine opened up and in pieces for repairs when the signal to raise steam was made. Chief Engine Room Artificer J. G. Hill was awarded the D.S.M. "for his smart performance in getting the port engine, which was disconnected, into working order." It will have been noticed that the ship was steaming 20 knots two and a half hours after the signal to raise steam. This was a remarkable performance, and reflected great credit on her entire engineering staff.

A signalman, Frank Glover, was given the D.S.M. for "carrying out his duties of range-taker in a very cool manner during the whole of the action." He was in an entirely exposed position on the fore upper bridge.

More has been said about the part taken by the *Cornwall*, as the writer was on board her, and most of the incidents described came under his personal observation. They are, however, typical of the conduct of the officers and men in the other ships that took part.[9]

CHAPTER XIII
THE SINKING OF THE "NÜRNBERG"

"While England, England rose,
Her white cliffs laughing out across the waves,
Victorious over all her enemies."
—Alfred Noyes (*Drake*).

We must now go back to the commencement of the action with the *Leipzig*. At 4.30 P.M., in accordance with a signal made by the *Cornwall*, the *Kent* branched off in pursuit of the *Nürnberg* and was soon out of sight.

Thus a third fight developed through the high speed attained by the *Kent*, which enabled her to catch up and force action on the *Nürnberg*. The following description has been largely compiled from a narrative written by an officer in the *Kent*, while from the particulars undernoted concerning the ships two important features stand out: the speed of the two ships was nearly equal, and the German was built five years later than her opponent, and therefore should have been able to maintain her speed with less difficulty.

Name	Tonnage	Armament	Speed	Completion
Kent	9,800	14—6"	23.7	1903
Nürnberg	3,396	10—4.1" 8—2.1"	23.5	1908

"Brassey's Naval Annual."

In the course of the afternoon the weather became misty, so that it seemed imperative to get to close quarters as rapidly as possible. That this was fully realised and acted upon is shown by what was written by an officer in the *Kent*: "In the last hour of the chase, helped by a light ship and a clean bottom, by the most determined stoking, by unremitting attention to her no longer youthful boilers—in short, by the devotion of every officer and man in the engine and boiler rooms, the *Kent* achieved the remarkable speed of 25 knots."

Both ships were steering a south-easterly course at 5 P.M. when the *Kent* got within range of the *Nürnberg*, which opened fire with her stern guns. The chase had in all lasted nearly seven hours, so the sound of the enemy's guns proved doubly welcome, since it brought home the fact that the German was now trapped. The fall of the enemy's shot was awaited with that eagerness combined with anxiety which only those who have undergone the experience can fully realise. Accurate ranges were hard to take on account of the abnormal vibration caused by the speed at which the ship was travelling, but it was expected that the enemy's first salvoes would fall short. But not a sign was to be seen anywhere of these projectiles. Where, then, had they gone?

Officers glanced round the horizon to make quite certain that the enemy was not firing at another ship, but nothing else was in sight. A light, drizzling rain was falling, so that it was not till the third salvo that the splashes were discovered astern of the ship. This bore out the experience of the *Cornwall* and *Glasgow*, which had also been astonished at the long range of the German 4.1" gun, which is said to be sighted up to 12 kilometres (13,120 yards).

Nine minutes after (5.9) the *Kent* opened fire at 11,000 yards with her fore turret, but the shots fell short. Altering course slightly to port, she was able to bring her two foremost 6-inch on the starboard side to bear, making four guns in all. The light was poor, and both ships had difficulty in seeing well enough to correct the gun range at this distance. Thus this opening stage of the combat was not very fruitful of results as far as could be judged, though survivors subsequently stated that the *Kent* scored two effective hits, one of which penetrated the after steering flat below the waterline and killed all the men in it with one exception. On the other hand, the enemy (missing mainly for deflection) only got in one hit during the same period.

About 5.35 two boilers of the *Nürnberg* burst in quick succession, apparently from excess of pressure due to her strenuous efforts to escape. This reduced her speed to 19 knots, when all hope of averting disaster, even with the aid of several lucky shots, was shattered at one fell swoop. The *Kent* now gained very rapidly on her opponent, and all anxiety as to the chase being prolonged until dark was dispelled.

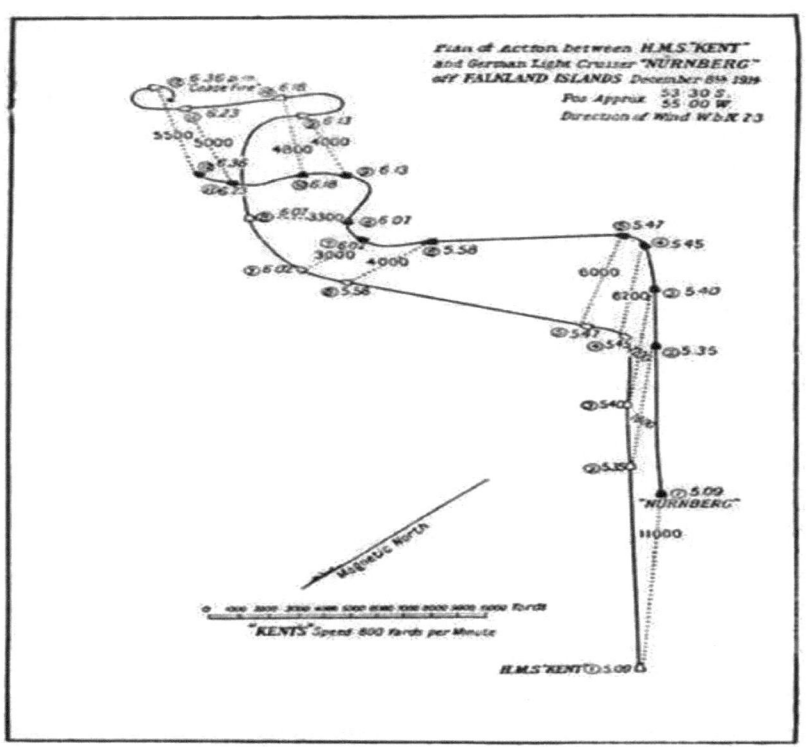

Plan of action between H.M.S. "KENT" and German Light Cruiser "NÜRNBERG" off FALKLAND ISLANDS December 8th 1914

Realising the hopelessness of continuing the attempt to escape, the German decided to fight it out, and altered course ten minutes later 90 degrees to port (see Plan). The Kent turned about 70 degrees to port, so that both ships were on converging courses, and able to bring every gun on the broadside to bear. The running fight was over, and the action developed during the ensuing quarter of an hour into as fierce a duel as it is possible to imagine, with the range rapidly decreasing from 6,000 to 3,000 yards and all guns firing in succession, keeping up one continuous thunder. The Kent now started using her lyddite shell. As was only to be expected, a good deal of damage resulted. In a very short time a fire broke out near the German's mainmast, followed a little later by the fall of her main-topmast, which bent gracefully forward like a sapling, and then fell with a crash. Both ships were firing their guns independently, not in salvoes, and in consequence the sequence of the discharges was almost unbroken. A fearful din resulted, which was as loud as it was penetrating, and soon began to have an irritating effect on the nerves. The incessant clanging and clashing jarred horribly and gave the impression that the ship was being continually hit; in fact, those below began to think that matters were not going too well from the constant concussions and severe jolts that were felt, until they were reassured by the optimistic and cheering bits of news passed down through the voice-pipes. The *Kent's* fore-topgallant-mast now suddenly fell over, fortunately remaining suspended in midair by the stays; a chance shot had cut right through the heel.

From the rate of fire maintained at such a short range it was patent that matters would soon be brought to a finish so far as the *Nürnberg* was concerned. By 6.5 P.M. her fore-topmast had disappeared, she was on fire in two or three places, and her speed was still further reduced. She turned away, as if to escape such heavy punishment, the details of which could be plainly observed at this short distance. Her upper deck was a veritable shambles, and most of the guns' crews, only protected by gun shields, had been killed. In the words of one of the *Kent's* officers, "her foretop and foremost funnel were so riddled that they appeared to be covered with men"; the torn and twisted steel sticking out in every direction caused this paradoxical illusion. Only two of her guns on the port side remained in action.

On the other hand, the *Kent* herself had by no means come out unscathed. In addition to the hits already mentioned, there were many more that had struck the ship's side and boat deck on the starboard side, but no fires of consequence had taken place, nor had there been any hits on the water-line of a vital character. One of the enemy's shells burst just outside the midship casemate situated on the main deck. Only fragments entered, but there were ten casualties, most of them burns; one man was killed instantly, and he remained in the same position after death with arms bent for holding a cordite charge. A small fire was caused, and the flames passed down the ammunition hoist to the passage below, igniting a charge which was hooked on ready to be hoisted. Had it not been for the prompt action of Sergeant Charles Mayes, of the Royal Marines, complete destruction might easily have followed. With the greatest presence of mind, he immediately isolated the cordite charges in the vicinity, closed the sliding scuttle in the hoist, and at the same time ordered his men to run for the nearest hoses to flood the compartment. The fire was extinguished before it could get a hold, and for this brave deed he was awarded the Conspicuous Gallantry Medal and an annuity of £20.

The *Nürnberg* executed a sudden and unexpected manœuvre at 6.10 by turning inwards as if about to ram her opponent. Continuing the turn, however, she eventually passed astern of the *Kent* and brought her starboard guns into play for the first time. During this manœuvre, and while in an end-on position, two of our shells burst almost simultaneously on her forecastle, causing a fire and putting the guns there out of action.

In reply to this manœuvre the *Kent* turned to a nearly opposite course. It will be realised from the plan that the *Kent* was travelling well over twice as fast as her opponent at this time, and that her port guns were now brought into action. The courses of both ships were again roughly parallel, the *Kent* taking care to avoid getting on the beam of the *Nürnberg*, which would have afforded the latter an opportunity of using her torpedoes.

From now on the distance between the two ships gradually increased.

The German's fire was very spasmodic, and it was evident that she could not last much longer. By 6.25 her engines were apparently stopped, for she was barely moving through the water. She was now badly battered and scarcely recognisable as the ship of an hour and a half before. The *Kent* had to turn right round again to keep somewhere near her, and continued to fire at her with devastating effect.

At 6.36 the enemy ceased fire altogether, the *Kent* followed suit, and for a short while awaited developments. Being now on fire all along her fore part, the German ship looked a complete wreck, and showed not a vestige of life as she lay helpless on the water. She had a list, and was at a dead standstill. In vain the *Kent* waited for her to strike her colours, and so, as she showed no signs of sinking, opened fire once more, slowly closing and keeping well before her beam, firing at her with all guns that would bear. Not till 6.57 did she haul down her colours, whereupon all firing ceased.

On examination it was found that nearly all the *Kent's* boats were splintered or smashed up by the enemy's fire, and there were only two that could be temporarily patched up in a short space of time. While the necessary repairs were in progress, the *Nürnberg*, which had been heeling over more and more, turned over on her starboard side, and in a deathlike silence disappeared beneath the surface at 7.27 P.M. Captain J. D. Allen, in Writing of his Men, says, "No sooner had she sunk than the *Kent's* men displayed the same zeal and activity in endeavouring to save life as they had done in fighting the ship. Boats were hastily repaired and lowered, manned by men eagerly volunteering to help. Unfortunately, the sea was rough and the water very cold, so we only succeeded in picking up twelve men, of whom five subsequently died." The search for the survivors was continued till 9 A.M. It is said that even the living were attacked by albatrosses.

While the ship was sinking a few German seamen gathered at the stern and waved their ensign to and fro before going down with the ship.

The *Kent* was hit thirty-seven times altogether, but suffered no damage affecting her seaworthiness. Her wireless telegraphy transmitting instruments were smashed to pieces by a shell, which passed through the wireless office. She was thus unable to report the result of her action, and caused the Commander-in-Chief some anxiety regarding her fate. The receiving instruments, however, were intact, so all the wireless signals made by the Commander-in-Chief inquiring as to her whereabouts were taken in and read, though she was powerless to reply. The upper works on the starboard side presented a sorry spectacle, but the armour, though hit, was unpierced. Only two shots burst against the unarmoured part of the ship's side, one making a hole about four feet square just before the foremost starboard 6-inch gun on the main deck, and the other a hole of about equal size on the same side immediately below the after shelter deck.

A German officer who was saved said that they had heard by wireless that the British had "blown up the harbour" at the Falklands, and had fled to the west coast of Africa! He also stated that the *Nürnberg* had not been refitted for three years, and that her boilers were in a very bad state, which was borne out by some of them having burst during the chase.

Each seaman 6-inch gun's crew had five Royal Naval Reservemen in it, and their conduct speaks volumes for the all-round efficiency of the men that the Navy has drawn from the Reserve during the War.

The total casualties in the *Kent* amounted to 16 men, 5 of whom were killed, whilst 3 of the wounded afterwards died of their wounds.

Commander Wharton, of the *Kent*, gives a remarkably realistic description of the closing scenes: "It was strange and weird all this aftermath, the wind rapidly arising from the westward, darkness closing in, one ship heaving to the swell, well battered, the foretop-gallant-mast gone. Of the other, nothing to be seen but floating wreckage, with here and there a man clinging, and the 'molly-hawks' swooping by. The wind moaned, and death was in the air. Then, see! Out of the mist loomed a great four-masted barque under full canvas. A great ghost-ship she seemed. Slowly, majestically, she sailed by and vanished in the night." This was the same ghost-ship that had appeared in the middle of the action fought by the battle-cruisers—a very fitting apparition, which upholds the legend that one always appears at a British naval engagement. Meeting one of the officers of this sailing vessel later on in the Dardanelles, it was revealed that she had been out at sea so long that she was unaware that war had even been declared, until she suddenly found herself a spectator of two naval actions on the same day.

A silk ensign, presented to the ship by the ladies of Kent, was torn to ribbons in the course of the day. The pieces, however, were carefully collected by Captain J. D. Allen, and returned to the donors, who sewed them together. This ensign now hangs in Canterbury Cathedral. A new silk ensign was given to the ship by the ladies of the county of Kent, and was hoisted on the first anniversary of the battle, December 8th, 1915.

CHAPTER XIV
AFTERMATH

... "England
Grasped with sure hands the sceptre of the sea,
That untamed realm of liberty which none
Had looked upon as aught but wilderness
Ere this, or even dreamed of as the seat
Of power and judgment and high sovereignty
Whereby all nations at the last should make
One brotherhood, and war should be no more."

—Alfred Noyes (*Drake*).

The battle of the Falkland Islands was, perhaps, more like the old-time naval engagements fought by sailing ships of the line than any other naval battle that is likely to take place nowadays. There were no submarines, no destroyers, no aeroplanes or Zeppelins, nor any other of the manifold death-dealing devices that tend to make war so much more hideous than in days gone by. In a word, it was open fighting. Not a torpedo was fired. Not even a mine was dropped, if the survivors who stated that the German ships did not carry them can be believed. There were a few anxious moments when zinc cases were seen floating on the surface ahead, glistening in the sunlight, but they turned out to be empty cartridge cases that the enemy had dropped overboard.

There were three very general feelings that followed on after the battle: firstly, that we had at last been able to achieve something of real value; secondly, that it was quite as good as a fortnight's leave (the most one usually gets in the Navy); and thirdly, that the war would now soon be over. In a similar manner, after a local success on land, the soldiers at the beginning of the war frequently hoped that it might bring matters to a conclusion. Thus do local events in war assume an exaggerated importance.

There can be no two opinions as to the decisive nature of this battle. In the course of a single day, the whole of this German squadron, together with two colliers, had been destroyed with the exception of the light cruiser

Dresden. A comparison of the difference in the casualties points not only to its decisiveness, but also to the success of Admiral Sturdee's dispositions and methods of bringing the enemy to action. It was a strategic victory.

The German Admiral found himself very much in the same position as Admiral Cradock at Coronel, with one important difference. Cradock sought action despite the many odds against him, whereas von Spee tried to run when he found he was outclassed. Sir Henry Newbolt puts the proposition admirably. After remarking that running is the game of the losing side, he says, "You have only to consider what it would have been worth to Germany to have had a Cradock flying his flag in the *Scharnhorst* on that December 8th. You can imagine him, when the great battle-cruisers came out of harbour, signalling, 'I am going to attack the enemy now,' and going straight to meet them at full speed. Their steam was not yet up—he could have closed them then and there. What a fight that would have been! No impotent scattering flight, no hours of burning misery, with ships turning this way and that, to bring their guns to bear upon an enemy beyond their reach; but a desperate short-range action with every shot telling—a chance of dealing the enemy a heavy blow before the end, and the certainty of leaving a great tradition to the Service."

Directly the *Gneisenau* was sunk, wireless signals were made by the Commander-in-Chief asking where the *Dresden* was last seen, and in what direction she was heading at that time. It will be recollected that she had the speed of our armoured cruisers and got clean away without firing a single round, having been last seen by the *Glasgow* steering away to the S.S.W. Later signals were made calling up the *Kent*, as no one knew what had happened to her, since she was last seen going after the *Nürnberg*. These calls were repeated again and again without result on account of her damaged wireless, and it was not till the afternoon of the following day that all anxieties were allayed by the *Kent* arriving at Port William, bringing with her the news of another brilliant success.

The problem of the moment, therefore, was to complete the victory by rounding up the *Dresden* as soon as possible. Should she escape now and take refuge in one of the innumerable inlets or channels that abound in the unsurveyed localities of the southern part of South America, clearly it would be a matter of great difficulty to catch her. With his characteristic energy, Admiral Sturdee did not lose a moment in following up his victory. The *Carnarvon* was despatched to escort the *Orama* and colliers coming south from the base to Port Stanley. The two battle-cruisers *Invincible* and *Inflexible* proceeded with all haste to Staten Island, and thence made a careful search for the *Dresden* in the numerous bays around Tierra del Fuego. The *Glasgow* was ordered to the Straits of Magellan in the hope that she might intercept her, whilst the *Bristol* searched for both the *Dresden* and the *Kent* to the southward of the Falklands. Owing to lack of coal, the *Cornwall* was obliged to return to harbour, and was the first ship to arrive there on December 9th; she was followed shortly afterwards by the *Kent*.

During the night of December 8th a thick fog came on, which made the navigation of those of our ships endeavouring to make land no easy matter. Magnetic compasses are apt to be considerably affected by gun-fire, and consequently the dead-reckoning positions of our ships were by no means to be relied upon, and were not sufficiently accurate to give confidence in approaching an indented coast like the east side of the Falklands.

Sad to relate, not a vestige of the *Dresden* was seen by any of our ships that were scattered in the search for her. She was careful to abstain from using her wireless, even though there must have been several German supply ships in the vicinity who would urgently require to be informed of the annihilation of their squadron. This quest entailed travelling at high speed, so shortage of coal and oil fuel forced our ships to return one by one. By the evening of December 11th the whole squadron had once again reassembled at the Falklands.

Congratulations now poured in from all parts of the world, and were promulgated by the Commander-in-Chief. The Governor of the Falkland Islands, the Hon. William Allardyce, C.M.G., visited the flagship and congratulated Admiral Sturdee, together with the whole of our squadron, in glowing terms on behalf of the colony. Admiral Sturdee issued an interesting Memorandum, which is given *in toto*, calling attention to the urgent necessity for completing the victory by running the *Dresden* to earth. These messages are given in Part III.

Casualties in any decisive modern naval engagement are frequently very one-sided, one fleet suffering enormous losses whilst the other escapes with comparative immunity. This battle proved no exception to this rule. In the British squadron, the *Invincible* and *Cornwall* had no casualties, though they both had a big share of hits. The *Carnarvon* and *Bristol* were untouched. The *Inflexible* had 1 man killed and 3 slightly wounded. The *Glasgow* had 1 man killed and 4 wounded through a single unlucky shot. The heaviest casualties occurred in the *Kent*, who had 5 men killed and 11 wounded, 3 of whom subsequently succumbed to their wounds; most of these were caused by the bursting of one shell. She was hit thirty-seven times, and went in to a much closer range than the remainder of our ships. The squadron, therefore, incurred a total loss of 10 men killed and 15 wounded, whilst the Germans lost some 2,260 men all told. The crews of their ships totalled 2,432 officers and men, and were estimated as follows:

Scharnhorst	872	*Gneisenau*	835
Nürnberg	384	*Leipzig*	341

The prize bounty amounted to the sum of £12,160, to be divided amongst the officers and crews of the *Invincible, Inflexible, Carnarvon, Cornwall, Kent,* and *Glasgow,* being calculated at the usual rate of £5 per head. In the course of the Prize Court proceedings the following reference to the German Admiral Count von Spee was made in regard to his action at Coronel: "Whatever others might have thought of this twist of the lion's tail, it appeared that the German Admiral was under no delusion.... It was perhaps as well to put on record that the German Admiral, when he took his fleet into Valparaiso, refused to drink the toast of 'Damnation to the British Navy,' and apparently had a premonition that his end was very near."

The prisoners of war were all sent home in the *Macedonia* and the storeship *Crown of Galicia,* but not before Admiral Sturdee had given them to understand in the firmest possible manner that if any man was found tampering with the ship's fittings, or was discovered out of that portion of the ship allocated to his use, he would be very severely dealt with.

The few days spent at Port Stanley after the battle will always live in the memory of those who were present. They were days full of hard work, combined with visits to friends and interesting discussions on individual experiences. The interest of meeting, boarding, and going over other ships to view the shot holes may be imagined. Reports and plans had to be made out. Several ships had to be heeled over to get at the damaged part, and presented a comic appearance, the *Cornwall* being so far over as to look positively dangerous. All ships had to coal and were busy at it night and day. Few will forget those night coalings—ugh!—in a temperature of forty degrees, with a bitterly cold wind accompanied almost invariably by occasional squalls of hail and rain.

Those cheers we gave one another will not be forgotten; they rang true, being full of pent-up enthusiasm, and, as Mr. John Masefield says, "went beyond the guard of the English heart."

Unfortunately, subsequent events have made it impossible to recall this overwhelming victory without a feeling of sadness due to the loss of the gallant *Invincible* in the battle of Jutland. One description of that battle says that four of her men succeeded in boarding a raft, and as one of our ships passed, taking them at first for Huns, the narrator adds, "The four got up on their feet and cheered like blazes. It was the finest thing I have ever seen." Most of her crew were lost, but we have at least the satisfaction of knowing they died as heroes.

CHAPTER XV
THE PSYCHOLOGY OF THE SAILOR IN ACTION

"Mother and sweetheart, England; ...
... thy love was ever wont
To lift men up in pride above themselves
To do great deeds which of themselves alone
They could not; thou hast led the unfaltering feet
Of even thy meanest heroes down to death,
Lifted poor knights to many a great emprise,
Taught them high thoughts, and though they kept their souls
Lowly as little children, bidden them lift
Eyes unappalled by all the myriad stars
That wheel around the great white throne of God."

—Alfred Noyes (*Drake*).

The naval man is often confronted with the question: "What does it feel like to be in an action at sea?" This is undoubtedly very difficult to answer in anything approaching an adequate manner. There are various reasons for hesitancy in reply. Broadly speaking, the answer depends on two main factors, environment and temperament, but there are many minor points depending on the experience, education, and character of the man in question that at the same time vitally affect it. An attempt to generalise, therefore, is sure to be open to criticism. It is consequently with much diffidence that the following ideas are set forth, in the hope that they may assist the landsman to appreciate, in some slight degree, the various points of view of the officers and men who fight in our warships.

There is obviously a wide difference in the outlook, and consequently in the working of the mind, of the man behind a gun, or in any other position where he can see and hear how matters are progressing, and the man buried in the bowels of the ship, who is stoking, working machinery, or engaged in the supply of ammunition. When once the action has begun, the former will probably never give a moment's thought to his own safety or that of the ship he is in, whilst the latter, during any intervals that may occur in his work, can only think of how things are going with his ship. Lastly, there is a very divergent view between the man who knows he is going into a battle such as that fought off the Falkland Islands, where our ships possessed a marked superiority, and the man who was present, say, at Coronel, where the conditions were reversed.

During an action, the captain of a man-of-war is usually in the conning-tower, where he is surrounded by several inches of steel. A good all-round view is obtained through a slit between the roof and the walls. From this point of vantage he can communicate with the gunnery control positions, the gun positions, engine-rooms, torpedo-rooms, and, in fact, with every portion of the complex machine represented by a modern warship. Having spent a number of years at sea, he has frequently pictured to himself what a naval engagement would be like, but it is very problematical whether he has ever taken the trouble to analyse what his own feelings would be; in any case, his imaginations were probably both far from the reality. When approaching the scene of action he most likely gives a passing thought to his kith and kin, but his responsibility will be too great to admit of his feelings taking hold of him, and his thoughts will afterwards be concentrated entirely on the work in hand. During the action he is watching every movement with the utmost keenness, giving a curt order where necessary as he wipes from his face the salt water splashed up by a short projectile. His nerves and even his muscles are strung up to a high pitch of tensity, and he loses himself altogether in working out the problem before him.

The gunnery officer in the control position on the foremast is, of course, in a much more exposed position; without any armour protection to speak of. Doubtless there flashes across his mind a hope that he will come through without being picked off by a stray shot. The thoughts of the men with him, and those of the men working the range-finders, who also have practically no protection, will probably be very similar to his. But when approaching the enemy, all their attention is needed to acquire as much information as possible, in order to get an idea of his approximate course and speed. Later, all their faculties are exercised in determining the corrections to be made to the sights of their guns as regards range and deflection, so as to hit the enemy, and in giving the orders to fire.

The navigation officer, notebook in hand, is with the captain in the conning-tower, and his thoughts are not far different. His attention is riveted on the course of the ship and any impending manœuvre that he may presume to be imminent or advisable. In some of the older ships, where the quartermaster steers from the conning-tower, his observation is often made more irksome by salt-water spray getting into his eyes and preventing him from seeing the compass clearly.

With the commander and others who may be below in the ammunition passages in the depths of the ship, the one thought obsessing the mind to the exclusion of almost everything else will be: "What is happening, and how are we getting on?" Passing up ammunition is no sinecure; it is invariably a warm job down below. Stripped to the waist, hard at it, and perspiring freely, many a joke is cracked in much the same spirit as inspires Tommy in the trenches. Now and again a bit of news comes down and is passed along like lightning from mouth to mouth. For example, in one case a shell hits one of our ship's funnels, and it has gone by the board with a frightful din, as if hell were suddenly let loose; the news is passed down to the commander in the ammunition passage, to which he cheerily replies: "That's all right; we have plenty left, haven't we?" Again, a shell strikes the hull of the ship, making her quiver fore and aft and almost stop her roll; naturally the effect of this is felt down below far more than on deck, and though some may wonder whether it has struck on the waterline or not, there is merely a casual remark that the enemy is shooting a bit better.

The engineer officers in the engine-rooms are constantly going to and fro along the greasy steel floors, watching every bearing and listening intently to every sound of the machinery in much the same way as a motorist listens to hear if his engine is misfiring. They, too, are longing for news of how the fight is going on as they keenly watch for any alteration of the engine-room telegraphs, or of the hundred and one dials showing the working of the various engines under their charge.

The stokers, stripped to a gantline, and digging out for daylight, are in much the same position as those passing up ammunition, save that they seldom, if ever, get a lull in their work in which to indulge their thoughts. Those trimming the coal in the boxlike bunkers have perhaps the most unenviable task. Breathing in a thick haze of coal dust, black from head to foot, they work on at full pressure in these veritable black holes, without the chance of hearing any news of what is going on "up topsides."

Every man in the ship is working at his appointed station during an action—even the cooks are busy assisting with the supply of ammunition—everyone is behind armour, or below the waterline, with the exception of those few whose duties do not permit of it. This fact accounts for the comparatively few casualties in the ships that come out the victors in a sea fight, in spite of the tremendous havoc done by a shell bursting in the vicinity of cast steel, which throws up multitudes of splinter in all directions.

The guns' crews are all working at their respective weapons, sometimes wading in water if a heavy swell falls short close to them. Yet they see the result of their work, and every bit of damage done to the enemy is invariably put down to the handiwork of their individual gun. They may be said to be having the time of their lives in a successful action. During a lull, the enemy's fire is heavily criticised; suggestions as to the corrections that should be applied to his gunsights in order to get a hit are calmly made as they watch the splashes of his projectiles, and are as soon contradicted by some other authority who suggests something different. When their own ship is hit a remark is made to the effect—"That was a good 'un!" from the coldly calculating point of view of the expert. Unaccountable as it may seem, during artillery fire at sea there is usually this irrepressible desire to figure out the corrections needed for the enemy's gunsights in order that he may register a direct hit. Several of our naval officers testified to this strange phenomenon at Gallipoli, when undergoing a bombardment from Turkish forts and batteries, and added that they were held fascinated in doing so.

On the other hand, when a shell goes beyond the ship, at the first shrill whiz-z-z overhead, one calculates deliberately that the enemy will shortly lower his range, and, discretion being the better part of valour, the welcome shelter of a turret, casemate, or conning tower is speedily sought. It is curious that if the shells are falling short there is no such concern for the safety of one's skin. The writer has seen a group of officers having a spirited argument as to the corrections that should be made to the sights of a Turkish gun whose shell fell a few hundred yards short of the ship. It was not till one screamed past their heads, pitching in the water on the far side, that they thought of taking cover. The analogy does not apparently hold good to the same extent in the sister Service, for on terra firma the range is registered with fair accuracy, and it is usual to scuttle off to a dug-out as soon as Beachy Bill or Long Tom opens fire.

A shell from a heavy gun whistling close overhead seems to recall something of the physical emotion experienced as a child, when one ventured too high in a swing. There is a sort of eerie feeling in the interior which seems to struggle upward to one's throat, thereby causing a throttling sensation; and this seems to take place continuously, though it diminishes slightly as time goes on.

Another feature that is perhaps worth mentioning is what the sailor calls "getting a cheap wash." This occurs incessantly in a naval action, for a large shell fired at a long range falling into the water close to a ship will throw up a solid wall of water, often two or three hundred feet in height, so that it is no uncommon thing to get frequently soused. In the Falkland Islands battle the men right up in the control tops on the masts of the battle-cruisers complained of being unable to work their instruments satisfactorily owing to frequent drenchings by spray.

The strain that is undergone during a naval action can easily be imagined, though most men will agree that they are unconscious of it at the time; it is not until everything is over and finished with that its effects materialise. In the Navy every officer and man bears the burden of responsibility, and frequently it is one upon which may depend the safety of the lives of his shipmates. He may have to execute a manœuvre of vital importance—close a watertight compartment, put out a fire caused by a high explosive shell— or do any of the hundred and one duties that are necessary in a man-of-war. Newton's law of gravitation tells us that to every action there is an equal and opposite reaction. This fundamental principle undoubtedly holds good in the working of the human mind. The old example that a piece of cord, gradually stretched tighter and tighter until its limit of elasticity is attained, sags when the force is removed, is a very good parallel indeed of what takes place during and after action so far as the average fighting man is concerned. His mind, and all his faculties, have been extended to their full capacity in concentrating on the work in hand, in seeing that there is no sign of a hitch anywhere, in forestalling any possible accident, and in thinking out his own line of action in any given circumstance that may arise. The man who has been toiling physically has also been strung up to the highest possible pitch; the very best that is in him has been called forth, and he has in all probability never done better work, or striven so hard in his life before.

The bugle call "Cease fire" does not necessarily imply that all is over; it may only mean a temporary cessation or lull in the action; but when the "Secure" is sounded, there is no mistaking that the fight is finished. This is followed by the "Disperse," when all guns are secured, ammunition returned, and all the magazines and shell rooms locked up. Then a large number of the men are free; orders are given to the engine-room department regarding the speed required, enabling some of the stokers told off as relief parties and employed in trimming coal to be released.

As a general rule, however, the guns are kept manned and speed is not reduced after a modern naval action, so that the number of men released from duty is comparatively small. Perhaps the enemy is sinking, when the seamen will be engaged in turning out boats preparatory to saving life. The men who are unemployed watch the sinking of an enemy ship with very different sentiments. All experience a glow of satisfaction, and most men will pity the poor wretches who are drowning or clinging more or less hopelessly to floating pieces of wreckage. A few are entirely callous, deeming such emotions a sign of weakness in view of the many atrocities committed by the enemy. This scarcely applied after the battle of the Falkland Islands, where the "Hymn of Hate" and other German propaganda fostering feelings of enmity had not embittered men's minds.

Lastly, there comes the utter physical weariness both of mind and body, attended by an intense longing for food, drink, and sleep, accompanied by the pleasant thought that the war will now soon be over. Officers crowd into the wardroom to get a drink and something to eat. The galley fire will be out, for the chef has been passing up ammunition, so no hot food, tea, or cocoa will be available for some little time. A walk round the ship reveals men lying in all sorts of impossible postures, too done up to bother about eating; others are crowding round the canteen, or getting any food that they can on the mess deck.

After the battle of the Falkland Islands one of the boy stewards who had been passing up shell during the action was found in the ammunition passage, "dead to the world," lying athwart an old washtub. There he was, in that stale and stuffy atmosphere, in the most uncomfortable position imaginable, fast asleep, completely worn out from sheer exhaustion, with his head and arms dangling over one side of the tub.

A large number have to continue their labours on watch in the engine room or on deck, in spite of having the greatest difficulty in keeping their eyes open. The extreme tension and strain is over, and it requires a strong effort to resist the temptation to let things slide and relapse into a state of inanition.

That the men brace themselves to grapple with their further duties in a spirit which allows no sign of reluctance or fatigue to show itself, does them infinite credit. They must look forward nevertheless to the moment when the ship will pass safely into some harbour guarded by net-defence from submarine attack, where all the guns' crews are not required to be constantly awake at their guns, and fires can be put out. Then, after coaling, prolonged and undisturbed sleep may be indulged in to make up for the lost hours, and "peace, perfect peace," will reign—for a while.

CHAPTER XVI
VON SPEE'S AIMS AND HOPES

The British Public and our gallant Allies have no doubt fully appreciated the commercial importance of the battle of the Falkland Islands. The relief that was thereby given to our shipping and trade not only in South American waters, but throughout our overseas Empire, can only be realised by those who have large interests therein. British trade with South America was first upset by the exploits of the *Karlsruhe*, later on prestige was still more affected by the Coronel disaster, and, finally, most of all by the expectation of the arrival of von Spee's squadron in the Atlantic. The freedom since enjoyed by our merchant shipping on all the sea-trade routes of the world was in great part due to the success of this portion of our Navy, the blockade having been firmly established by our powerful fleet in home waters. The toll of ships sunk and captured in the early months of the war would have been much greater, trade would have been seriously dislocated for the time being, and the pinch of a shortage in food supplies would probably have been felt had it not been for this very opportune victory.

What were von Spee's intentions after the destruction of Admiral Cradock's squadron we shall probably never know, but it is evident that he could not remain in the Pacific; it is fairly certain, also, that he intended to seize the Falkland Islands if he found them insufficiently guarded, as he had reason to infer was the case. Obviously the most tempting course then open to him, whether he took the Falklands or not, was to hold up our trade along the whole of the east coast of South America. But the possibility of doing this was diminished by his fatal delay after Coronel, before making a move. Had he acted at once he might have been able to do this with impunity for at least a month, by dividing up his squadron into small units. His coal and other supplies would have been easily assured through the armed merchant cruisers *Prinz Eitel Friedrich* and *Kronprinz Wilhelm*, organising the colliers and shoreships along these coasts. The *Kronprinz Wilhelm* had been operating for months past on the north coast of South America in conjunction with the *Karlsruhe*, and therefore already knew the tricks of this trade.

Had he been permitted to pursue this policy, von Spee was inevitably bound to touch on the delicate subject of neutrality in arranging supplies for so numerous a squadron. Now, according to the laws laid down by Article 5 of the Hague Conference, 1907, "belligerents are forbidden to use neutral ports and waters as a base of operations against their adversaries." By Article 12 it is laid down that in default of any other special provisions in the legislation of a neutral Power, belligerent warships are forbidden to remain in the ports, roadsteads, or territorial waters of the said Power for more than twenty-four hours, except in special cases covered by the Convention. It is left to the neutral to make regulations as to the hospitality it will afford, and those laid down by Brazil were that a belligerent vessel was only allowed to visit one of their ports once in three months for the purpose of obtaining supplies.

Being aware of these conditions, and that neutrality could not be imposed upon to an unlimited extent, it follows that von Spee would have been dependent in a great measure on supply ships which were able to evade the scrutiny of the neutral authorities—a precarious state of existence. Coal would be his prime necessity, and he might have hoped to secure a supply of this from captured colliers, but he could not depend upon it for such a large number of ships. Meanwhile, however, very considerable damage might have been done to our shipping, and it is generally believed the Germans were optimistic enough to hope that England would be brought to her knees from starvation by being cut off from both North and South American ports during this period, although there was really no ground whatsoever for such a surmise. Perhaps we shall in the future be careful not to frame so many laws for the conduct of war, since the Power that neglects these laws rides roughshod over her more conscientious opponent.

Such a scheme may have been the natural outcome of von Spee's success at Coronel. On the other hand, it is impossible to state with certainty that he did not intend to go ultimately to the Cape of Good Hope or some other part of Africa, but the pros and cons have already been discussed, and it scarcely appears probable. Von Spee, of course, had no notion of the prompt measure taken by our Admiralty in dispatching two powerful battle-cruisers of high speed to these waters without loss of time and in complete secrecy, though he must have concluded that no time would be lost in sending out reinforcements. Apparently his judgment was here at fault; hence the proposed attack on our colony in the Falkland Islands, the capture of which would have yielded him coal for his squadron's immediate requirements.

Von Spee is said to have been over-persuaded by his staff to undertake this latter venture. His movements here certainly led to the conclusion that he had no fixed plan. When the *Invincible* reached Pernambuco on her way home, there was a strong rumour that three colliers had been waiting off the coast for the *Scharnhorst* and *Gneisenau*; this points to the capture of the

Falklands not being included in the original plan. Admiral Sturdee searched the area for these ships but found nothing.

Both the British and German squadrons refrained from using wireless, and so had no knowledge of their proximity during the first week in December. Had the German ships passed our squadron whilst coaling at the Falklands, they would in all likelihood have separated, and would then have had a free hand—for some time, at any rate—along the east coast, whilst our ships would have gone round the Horn and searched for them in vain in the Pacific. The first intimation of their having eluded our squadron would have been that much of our shipping would be reported overdue in England from South American ports (for von Spee would most assuredly have avoided approaching within sight of land). This would very probably have been put down in the first few instances to the depredations of the *Karlsruhe*, whose fate was at this time quite unknown. The *Scharnhorst* and *Gneisenau* were sufficiently powerful to cope with anything which von Spee thought was likely to be in these seas. As a matter of fact, however, the battle-cruiser *Princess Royal* was in North American waters at this time, having left England in secrecy soon after the *Invincible* and *Inflexible* were dispatched south.

In further support of this theory of what was the German Admiral's plan of campaign, it may be mentioned that a fully laden German collier was forced to intern at a South American port south of the Plate in order to avoid capture by the *Carnarvon* and *Cornwall*, who were searching the coast there just after the battle of the Falklands took place. Another collier, the *Mera*, put back into Montevideo very hurriedly and interned herself, and lastly, the tender *Patagonia* ended her career in like manner. The presence of all these ships in this locality is evidence of the organisation arranged for the supply of the German squadron along this coast, and precludes the idea of its going to Africa.

There is evidence to show that von Spee picked up naval reservists for his squadron at Valparaiso, but there is none to confirm the rumour that he proposed to occupy the Falkland Islands, retaining a garrison there after they had been captured. He could never have hoped to occupy or to hold them for any length of time. Baron von Maltzhan, the manager of a large sheep farm in Chile, was selected to take command of an expedition consisting of an armed force of some 500 men, whose function was to assist in the capture of the Falkland Islands, but not necessarily to remain on as a permanent garrison.

The damage that can be done to merchant shipping and trade by a single hostile ship has been demonstrated on more than one occasion during this war. If, therefore, it is presumed that the revised German programme was to capture the Falkland Islands, thus aiming a blow at British prestige, and then to scatter in the manner suggested so as to hamper or cripple our trade with the New World as long as possible, it will then be seen how opportune a victory this was for the British nation.

Had von Spee escaped being brought to action, it seems probable that he would have endeavoured to work his way home in preference to the alternative of internment.

In brief, then, this is a rough outline of events that "might"—one could almost use the word "would"—have taken place, had not such prompt steps been taken by the Admiralty to meet him wherever he went by superior forces. Von Spee knew he was being cornered, and is reported to have said so at Valparaiso.

If additional proof of the decision of the Germans to bring about this war, whatever the cost, were required, it is to be found in the testimony of a captured German reservist, who has already been mentioned in this book. He was German interpreter to the Law Courts at Sydney. This man told a naval surgeon who was examining him after he had been rescued, when he was still in a very shaken condition and could have had no object in lying, that he had been called up by the German Admiralty on *June 26th*. In company with several other reservists, therefore, he took passage in a sailing ship bound for Valparaiso, where he ultimately joined the *Leipzig*. This tale is corroborated by the fact that von Spee put into Valparaiso to pick up naval reservists in accordance with instructions from Germany, which perhaps may have been the cause of his delay in coming round the Horn after defeating Admiral Cradock. Other prisoners informed us that they had been cruising up and down the Chilean coast in order to meet a storeship from Valparaiso with these reservists on board, so as to avoid being reported. The latter, however, never turned up, so the Germans were obliged to put in there a second time.

The murder of the Archduke Francis Ferdinand of Austria and of his wife, the alleged cause of this war, took place at Serajevo, the capital of Bosnia, two days after this man was called up by German Admiralty orders, namely, on Sunday, June 28th, 1914.

A German newspaper, in speaking of the success of Admiral von Spee at Coronel, also admirably sums up the issue of the battle of the Falkland Islands: "The superiority of our fleet in no way detracts from the glory of our victory, for the very essence of the business of a strategist is the marshalling of a superior fleet at the right place and at the right moment."

"Not unto us,"

Cried Drake, "not unto us—but unto Him
Who made the sea, belongs our England now!
Pray God that heart and mind and soul we prove
Worthy among the nations of this hour
And this great victory, whose ocean fame
Shall wash the world with thunder till that day
When there is no more sea, and the strong cliffs
Pass like a smoke, and the last peal of it
Sounds thro' the trumpet."

                                        Alfred Noyes (*Drake*).

CHAPTER XVII
THE PARTING OF THE WAYS

"Now to the Strait Magellanus they came
And entered in with ringing shouts of joy.
Nor did they think there was a fairer strait
In all the world than this which lay so calm
Between great silent mountains crowned with snow,
Unutterably lonely
From Pole to Pole, one branching bursting storm
Of world-wide oceans, where the huge Pacific
Roared greetings to the Atlantic."

Alfred Noyes (Drake).

The failure to round up the *Dresden* directly after the battle was naturally a great disappointment, but our recent success prevented anyone from feeling it too keenly. Hearing that the *Dresden* had suddenly put into Punta Arenas (Magellan Straits) to coal, Admiral Sturdee immediately ordered the *Inflexible*, *Glasgow*, and *Bristol* to go in pursuit of her in that direction. Sailing at 4 A.M. on December 13th, the *Bristol* arrived there the following afternoon to find that the *Dresden* had left the previous evening at 10 P.M., steaming away westwards. It was tantalising to have got so close to her, for she was not heard of again for months after this. All our ships now joined in the search, during which every possible bay and inlet was thoroughly examined. A glance at a large-scale map of this locality will show the difficulties that had to be surmounted. There were thousands of possible hiding-places amongst the channels and islands, many of which were quite unsurveyed; and, at first sight, it appeared nearly impossible to investigate all of these in anything short of a lifetime.

The Admiralty now ordered the *Invincible* to go to Gibraltar. On leaving harbour on the 14th, the *Cornwall* gave her a rousing send-off by "cheering ship," to which she enthusiastically replied. Admiral Sturdee sailed from Port Stanley on December 16th, to the great regret of the remainder of the squadron. He called in at Montevideo, Rio de Janeiro, and Pernambuco *en route,* and was received in almost the same spirit in which Nelson was acclaimed by the Ligurian Republic at Genoa in 1798.

Rear-Admiral Stoddart in the *Carnarvon* now took over the command of our squadron. The *Inflexible* continued the search for some days, after which she also was ordered off and sailed for the Mediterranean on December 24th. The remainder of our ships were scattered on both sides of South America and around Cape Horn.

Few people have the opportunity of realising the beauty and grandeur of the scenery in this part of the world, which resembles nothing so much as the fjords of Norway in the winter time. The depth of water allows ships to navigate the narrowest channels, where glacier-bounded mountains rise precipitously from the waters edge. Once on rounding a headland we came upon a most unusual sight: some forty albatrosses were sitting on the water. Our arrival caused them considerable inconvenience and alarm, and it was the quaintest sight to see these huge birds with their enormous spread of wing endeavouring to rise, a feat which many of them were unable to achieve even after several attempts. All these "fjords" abound in seals—chiefly of the hairy variety—sea-lions, and every imaginable kind of penguin. Long ropes of seaweed, usually known amongst the seafaring world as kelp, grow on the submerged rocks, and are an invaluable guide to the sailor as they indicate the rocky patches. They grow to an enormous length, and are to be seen floating on the face of the water; in fact, we had many an anxious though profitable moment in these unsurveyed localities owing to their sudden and unexpected appearance. At intervals a sliding glacier would enshroud the face of a mountain in a dense mist formed by myriads of microscopic particles of ice, which would be followed by wonderful prismatic effects as the sun forced his way through, transforming the scene into a veritable fairyland of the most gorgeous lights and shades. Towards sunset the rose-pink and deep golden shafts of light on the snow-covered peaks beggared all description, and forced the onlooker literally to gasp in pure ecstasy. Only the pen of a brilliant word-painter could do justice to the wealth of splendour of this ever-changing panorama.

The true Patagonian is nearly extinct, and the Indians inhabiting Tierra del Fuego are of a low social order, very primitive, and wild in appearance. We sometimes passed some of these in their crude dug-out canoes, which they handle most dexterously. Considering the severity of the climate, the temperature of which runs round about 40° Fahr., they wear remarkably few clothes, and the children frequently none at all, which accounts for the hardiness of those that survive.

The difference between the east and west territory of the Straits of Magellan is very marked. The Atlantic end is bordered by sandy beaches and green, undulating slopes backed by mountains, and the weather at this time of year is generally fine and calm; whereas the Pacific side is devoid of all vegetation, glaciers and mountain crags covered with snow descend nearly perpendicularly to the Straits, and it is no exaggeration to say that it is possible to go almost close alongside these high walls without any damage to the ship. Here the weather is altogether different, frequent blizzards are attended by rough weather, with heavy seas off the entrance, and it is far colder. The cause of this contrast lies in the Andes, which extend down to Cape Horn and break the force of the strong westerly winds (the roaring forties) that prevail in these latitudes.

On Christmas Day, 1914, the two battle-cruisers were on their way to Europe. The *Carnarvon* spent the day coaling in Possession Bay in the Straits of Magellan. We were also there in the *Cornwall*, but were more fortunate in having finished coaling the previous evening; however, we went to sea during the afternoon. It was scarcely what one would term a successful day, for the ship had to be cleaned, and it was impossible to decorate the mess deck, as is the custom. Nevertheless, we had a cheerful Service, which was followed by Holy Communion, and for the mid-day dinner there was plenty of salt pork and plum-duff! Unfortunately, as has been related, we were not to get our mail or our plum-puddings for many a long day. The *Kent, Glasgow, Bristol*, and *Orama* had poor weather off the coast of Chile, which did not help to enliven their Christmas. The *Otranto*, perhaps, was the best off, having recently come from Sierra Leone, where she had filled up with provisions.

The *Cornwall* was the next ship to be ordered away. We left Port Stanley on January 3rd, 1915, and sailed for England to have the damage to our side properly repaired in dry dock.

It would be tedious to follow in detail the wanderings of the remainder of our ships, who proceeded with colliers in company to ferret out every nook and cranny in this indented coastline. The *Newcastle* and some Japanese cruisers operated farther to the north along the Pacific side. Admiral Stoddart's squadron must have covered many thousands of miles with practically no respite in this onerous and fatiguing duty. Their lot was by no means enviable, they were perpetually under way, except when they stopped to replenish with coal, their mails were of necessity very irregular, and they were seldom able to get fresh food. Imagine, then, with what joy they ultimately found the termination of their labours in the sinking of the *Dresden*!

CHAPTER XVIII
THE LAST OF THE "DRESDEN"

"Tell them it is El Draque," he said, "who lacks
The time to parley; therefore it will be well
They strike at once, for I am in great haste."
There, at the sound of that renowned name,
Without a word down came their blazoned flag!
Like a great fragment of the dawn it lay,
Crumpled upon their decks....

Alfred Noyes (*Drake*).

There is remarkably little to tell about this action, which concludes the exploits of our ships in these waters. The whole fight only lasted a few minutes altogether—a poor ending to a comparatively fruitless career, considering the time that the *Dresden* was at large. During the months of January and February, 1915, the search for her had been carried on unremittingly; but though she had managed successfully to evade us, she was so pressed that she was unable to harass or make attacks on our shipping. That she never once attempted to operate along the main trade routes shows the energy with which this quest was prosecuted. From the time of her escape on December 8th till the day on which she sank, the *Dresden* only destroyed two sailing vessels. She, however, made such thorough arrangements to cover her movements that no reliable information as to her whereabouts ever leaked through to our squadron. Rumours were legion, and there were "people who were prepared to swear that they had seen her." The two places they mentioned were practically uncharted and were found to be full of hidden dangers. Acting on this "reliable" information, the localities were examined by our cruisers early in March, but it was found out afterwards that the *Dresden* had never visited either of them.

The armed merchantman *Prinz Eitel Friedrich* had been much more successful, and had captured and destroyed ten ships during these two months. Many, it is true, were sailing vessels, but none the less anxiety began to make itself felt in local shipping circles, and the whole position once more became uneasy and disturbed. Early in March the *Prinz Eitel Friedrich* arrived at Newport News in the United States with a number of prisoners on board, which had been taken from these prizes. She was badly in need of refit, and her engines required repairs. On learning that one of her victims was an American vessel, public indignation was hotly aroused, and but little sympathy was shown for her wants. Her days of marauding were brought to an end, for the Americans resolutely interned her.

On March 8th the *Kent*, in the course of her patrol duties, sighted the *Dresden* in latitude 37 S., longitude 80 W. It was a calm, misty morning, which made it impossible to see any distance. During the afternoon the haze suddenly lifted, and there was the *Dresden*, only ten miles away. The *Kent* seems to have sighted the *Dresden* first, and steamed full speed towards her for a few minutes before being observed. This interval, however, did not allow her to get within gun range. Of course the *Dresden*, being a far newer and faster vessel, soon increased the distance between them, and after a five-hours' chase, finally escaped under cover of the darkness. This was the first time she had been sighted by a British warship since December 8th. It was noticed that she was standing well out of the water, and this chase must have used up a lot of coal. It was obvious, therefore, that she would require coal very shortly, and at a no very distant port.

The *Kent* proceeded to Coronel to coal, informing the *Glasgow* and *Orama*. A search was organised, and, as a result of a wireless signal from the *Glasgow*, the *Kent* rejoined her not far from where the *Dresden* had been sighted. The *Glasgow*, *Kent*, and *Orama* caught sight of their quarry at 9 A.M. on March 14th, 1915, near Juan Fernandez Island. Smoke was seen to be issuing from the *Dresden's* funnels as our ships closed in on her from different directions. She was taken completely by surprise, and it was evident that there was no possible escape for her. As our ships approached she kept her guns trained on them, but did not attempt to open fire. Then all three British ships fired together, to which the German replied. The official statement tersely reports: "An action ensued. After five minutes' fighting the *Dresden* hauled down her colours and displayed the white flag."

Immediately the white flag was hoisted, all the British ships ceased firing. The crew of the *Dresden* then began to abandon her in haste, and were to be seen assembling on shore. Just as the last party of men were leaving the ship, the Germans made arrangements to blow up the foremost magazine. Not long afterwards there was a loud explosion, and the ship began to sink slowly, bows first. The *Dresden's* officers and men had all got well clear of the ship. An hour later, at a quarter-past twelve, she disappeared below the surface, flying the white flag and the German ensign which had been rehoisted at the last. All the surgeons and sick-berth staff of the British ships now attended to the German wounded, who were afterwards conveyed in the *Orama* to Valparaiso, where they were landed and taken to the German hospital.

Such a tame finish to their labours naturally caused disappointment amongst our ship's companies, who expected the enemy to uphold the traditions of Vice-Admiral von Spee by fighting to the last. The main object, however, had been achieved, the victory gained by Admiral Sturdee at the battle of the Falkland Islands had at last been made complete, and our ships in South American waters were now free to proceed on other useful service.

PART III
OFFICIAL DISPATCHES

I
DISPATCH OF THE ACTION OF H.M.S. "CARMANIA"

September 14th, 1914

The Secretary of the Admiralty communicates the following for publication. It is a narrative of the action in South Atlantic on September 14th, 1914, between H.M.S. *Carmania* and the German armed merchant ship *Cap Trafalgar*:—

Shortly after 11 A.M. we made out a vessel, and on nearer approach we saw there were three vessels, one a large liner, the others colliers. The latter had derricks topped, and were probably working when we hove in sight. Before we had raised their hulls they had separated, and were making off in different directions. The large vessel was, apparently, about our own size, with two funnels painted to represent a Castle liner. After running away for a little while, the large steamer turned to starboard and headed towards us. She was then steering about south, and we were steering about southwest. The weather was fine and sunny, with a moderate breeze from the north-east. Our speed was 16 knots, and his apparently about 18. At 8,500 yards we fired a shot across his bows, and he immediately opened fire from his starboard after gun. We opened with all the port guns, and the firing became general. We were now well within range, and most of his shots went over. Consequently our rigging, masts, funnels, derricks, and ventilators all suffered. He was then well open on our port side. All our port guns and his starboard guns engaged, and firing became rapid. Owing to the decreasing range, his machine guns were becoming particularly dangerous, so the ship was turned away from him and the range opened. The ship continued to turn until the starboard battery was engaged.

Two of our hits were seen to take his deck steam pipes. He was well on fire forward, and had a slight list to starboard. One of his shells had passed through the cabin, under our forebridge, and although it did not burst, it started a fire which became rapidly worse, no water being available owing to the fire main having been shot through. The chemical fire extinguishers proving of very little use, the fire got such a firm hold that the forebridge had to be abandoned, and the ship conned from aft, using the lower steering position. At this time the enemy was on our starboard, with a heavy list to starboard, and at 1.50 P.M., or one hour and forty minutes from the firing of the first shot, she capsized to starboard and went down bows first, with colours flying. It was some time before we got the fire under, which necessitated keeping the ship before the wind, and consequently we could not go to the assistance of the survivors, some of whom got away in boats and were picked up by one of the colliers.

The enemy before sinking was in wireless communication with some German vessel, and as smoke was seen in the northern horizon and the signalman thought he could make out a cruiser's funnels, we went off full speed to the southward. When we were in touch with the *Cornwall* all we asked him was to meet us, as the ship was unseaworthy and practically all communications and navigational instruments were destroyed, rendering the conning and navigation of the ship difficult and uncertain.

On the 15th, at 4.30 P.M., the *Bristol* picked us up and escorted us until relieved by the *Cornwall*, who took us on to an anchorage to effect temporary repairs.

The following were decorated for their services during this engagement:

Captain Noel Grant, Royal Navy, awarded the C.B. He commanded and manœuvred the *Carmania* throughout the action, and handled the ship with rare skill and judgment.

Acting-Commander James C. Barr, Royal Naval Reserve, awarded the C.B. He was primarily concerned in getting the fire under, and prevented it spreading.

Lieutenant-Commander E. L. B. Lockyer, Royal Navy, awarded the D.S.O. Controlled the gun-fire in the most cool and efficient manner, after which he concentrated all his energy on extinguishing the fire.

Chief Gunner Henry Middleton, Royal Navy, awarded the D.S.C. Did extremely well in charge of the ammunition parties, and encouraged his men by his personal behaviour and coolness.

Acting Sub-Lieutenant G. F. Dickens, Royal Naval Reserve, awarded the D.S.C. Saved vital parts of the Standard Compass when the bridge was abandoned, and then assisted in saving the charts.

Midshipman D. N. Colson, Royal Naval Reserve, awarded the D.S.C. Took the fire-hose into the Chart House, and in spite of being burned by falling wood, managed to pass the charts out to Sub-Lieutenant Dickens.

Lieutenant-Commander W. J. O'Neil and Lieutenant P. A. Murchie, of the Royal Naval Reserve, together with Chief-Engineer F. Drummond and 2nd Engineer J. Mcdonald, were all specially mentioned in dispatches.

In addition to the above, twelve men were awarded the D.S.M. for various acts of gallantry.

II
DISPATCH OF THE ACTION FOUGHT OFF CORONEL

November 1st, 1914

THE NAVAL FIGHT OFF CHILE

The Secretary of the Admiralty announces that the following report has been received from H.M.S. *Glasgow* (Captain John Luce, R.N.) concerning the recent action off the Chilean coast:—

Glasgow left Coronel 9 A.M. on November 1 to rejoin *Good Hope* (flagship), *Monmouth*, and *Otranto* at rendezvous. At 2 P.M. flagship signalled that apparently from wireless calls there was an enemy ship to northward. Orders were given for squadron to spread N.E. by E. in the following order: *Good Hope, Monmouth, Otranto,* and *Glasgow*, speed to be worked up to 15 knots. 4.20 P.M. saw smoke; proved to be enemy ships, one small cruiser and two armoured cruisers. *Glasgow* reported to Admiral, ships in sight were warned, and all concentrated on *Good Hope*. At 5 P.M. *Good Hope* was sighted.

5.47 P.M., squadron formed in line-ahead in following order: *Good Hope, Monmouth, Glasgow, Otranto*. Enemy, who had turned south, were now in single line-ahead 12 miles off, *Scharnhorst* and *Gneisenau* leading. 6.18 P.M., speed ordered to 17 knots, and flagship signalled *Canopus*, 'I am going to attack enemy now.' Enemy were now 15,000 yards away and maintained this range, at the same time jambing wireless signals.

By this time sun was setting immediately behind us from enemy position, and while it remained above horizon we had advantage in light, but range too great. 6.55 P.M., sun set, and visibility conditions altered, our ships being silhouetted against afterglow, and failing light made enemy difficult to see.

7.3 P.M., enemy opened fire 12,000 yards, followed in quick succession by *Good Hope, Monmouth, Glasgow*. Two squadrons were now converging, and each ship engaged opposite number in the line. Growing darkness and heavy spray of head sea made firing difficult, particularly for main deck guns of *Good Hope* and *Monmouth*. Enemy firing salvo got range quickly, and their third salvo caused fire to break out on fore part of both ships, which were constantly on fire till 7.45 P.M. 7.50 P.M., immense explosion occurred on *Good Hope* amidships, flames reaching 200 feet high. Total destruction must have followed. It was now quite dark.

Both sides continued firing at flashes of opposing guns. *Monmouth* was badly down by the bow and turned away to get stern to sea, signalling to *Glasgow* to that effect. 8.30 P.M., *Glasgow* signalled to *Monmouth*, 'Enemy following us,' but received no reply. Under rising moon enemy's ships were now seen approaching, and as *Glasgow* could render *Monmouth* no assistance, she proceeded at full speed to avoid destruction. 8.50 P.M., lost sight of enemy. 9.20 P.M., observed 75 flashes of fire, which was no doubt final attack on *Monmouth*.

Nothing could have been more admirable than conduct of officers and men throughout. Though it was most trying to receive great volume of fire without chance of returning it adequately, all kept perfectly cool, there was no wild firing, and discipline was the same as at battle practice. When target ceased to be visible, gunlayers spontaneously ceased fire. The serious reverse sustained has entirely failed to impair the spirit of officers and ship's company, and it is our unanimous wish to meet the enemy again as soon as possible.

III
OFFICIAL DISPATCH OF VICE-ADMIRAL COUNT VON SPEE

The following official report of the action fought off Coronel on November 1st appeared in the German Press, and is interesting in the light of being an accurate account as viewed by our enemies.

On comparing it with Captain Luce's account, it will be seen that the German clocks were about thirty minutes slow on our time. Other evidence also points to this conclusion:—

> The squadron under my command, composed of the large cruisers *Scharnhorst* and *Gneisenau*, and the small cruisers *Nürnberg, Leipzig*, and *Dresden*, reached on November 1st a point about twenty sea miles from the Chilean coast, in order to attack a British cruiser which, according to trustworthy information, had reached the locality on the previous evening. On the way to the spot the small cruisers were several times thrown out on the flanks to observe steamers and sailing ships.
>
> At 4.15 P.M. the *Nürnberg*, which was detached on one of these missions, was lost sight of to the north-east, while the *Dresden* remained about twelve sea miles behind. With the bulk of the fleet, I was about forty miles north of Arauco Bay. At 4.17 P.M. there were sighted to the south-west at first two ships, and then at 4.25 P.M. a third ship about fifteen miles away. Two of them were identified as warships, and were presumed to be the *Monmouth* and *Glasgow*, while the third was evidently the auxiliary cruiser *Otranto*. They, too, seemed to be on a southerly course. The squadron steamed at full speed in pursuit, keeping the enemy four points to the starboard. The wind was south, force 6, with a correspondingly high sea, so that I had to be careful not to be manœuvred into a lee position. Moreover, the course chosen helped to cut off the enemy from the neutral coast.

About 4.35 P.M. it was seen that the enemy ships were steering to the west, and I gradually changed my course south-west, the *Scharnhorst* working up 22 knots, while the *Gneisenau* and the *Leipzig* slowed down. The enemy's numerous wireless messages were 'jammed' as far as possible.

At 5.20 the arrival of another warship was reported which took the head of the line, and was identified as the *Good Hope*, the flagship of Rear-Admiral Cradock.

The enemy ships now got into battle formation, hoisted their mast-head flags, and tried slowly to approach a southerly course. From 5.35 P.M. onwards I held to a south-westerly course, and later to southerly course, and reduced speed to enable my own ships to come up. At 6.7 both lines—except *Dresden*, which was about one mile astern, and the *Nürnberg*, which was at a considerable distance—were on an almost parallel southerly course, the distance separating them being 135 hectometres (14,760 yards).

At 6.20, when at a distance of 124 hectometres, I altered my course one point towards the enemy, and at 6.34 opened fire at a range of 104 hectometres. There was a head wind and sea, and the ships rolled and pitched heavily, particularly the small cruisers, on both sides.

Observation and range-finding work was most difficult, the seas sweeping over the forecastles and conning-towers, and preventing the use of some guns on the middle decks, the crews of which were never able to see the sterns of their opponents, and only occasionally their bows. On the other hand, the guns of the two armoured cruisers worked splendidly, and were well served.

At 6.39 the first hit was recorded in the *Good Hope*. Shortly afterwards the British opened fire. I am of opinion that they suffered more from the heavy seas than we did. Both their armoured cruisers, with the shortening range and the failing light, were practically covered by our fire, while they themselves, so far as can be ascertained at present, only hit the *Scharnhorst* twice and the *Gneisenau* four times. At 6.53, when at a distance of 60 hectometres, I sheered off a point.

The enemy's artillery at this time was firing more slowly, while we were able to observe numerous hits. Among other things, it was seen that the roof of the fore double turret was carried away, and that a fierce fire was started in the turret. The *Scharnhorst* reckons thirty-five hits on the *Good Hope*.

As the distance, in spite of our change of course, had now decreased to 49 hectometres, it was to be presumed that the enemy doubted the success of his artillery, and was manœuvring for torpedo firing. The position of the moon, which had risen about six o'clock, favoured this manœuvre. At about 7.45, therefore, I gradually sheered off. In the meantime, darkness had set in, and the range-finders in the *Scharnhorst* for the moment used the reflections of the fires which had broken out in the *Good Hope* to estimate the distances; gradually, however, range-finding and observation became so difficult that we ceased fire at 7.26.

At 7.23 a big explosion was observed between the funnels of the *Good Hope*. So far as I could see, the ship did not fire after that. The *Monmouth* seems to have stopped firing at 7.20.

The small cruisers, including the *Nürnberg*, which came up in the meantime, were by 'wireless' at 7.30 to pursue the enemy and make a torpedo attack. At this time rain squalls limited the range of vision. The small cruisers were not able to find the *Good Hope*, but the *Nürnberg* came upon the *Monmouth*, which, badly damaged, crossed her bows and tried to come alongside. At 8.58 the *Nürnberg* sank her by a bombardment at point-blank range.

The *Monmouth* did not reply, but she went down with her flag flying. There was no chance of saving anybody owing to the heavy sea, especially as the *Nürnberg* sighted smoke, and believed that another enemy ship was approaching, which she prepared to attack.

At the beginning of the fight the *Otranto* made off. The *Glasgow* was able to keep up her harmless fire longer than her consorts maintained theirs, and she then escaped in the darkness.

The *Leipzig* and the *Dresden* believe that they hit her several times. The small cruisers sustained neither loss of life nor damage. The *Gneisenau* had two slightly wounded. The crews went into the fight with enthusiasm. Every man did his duty, and contributed to the victory.

IV
DISPATCH OF THE BATTLE OF THE FALKLAND ISLANDS

December 8th, 1914

ADMIRAL STURDEE'S DISPATCH

Admiralty, 3rd March, 1915.

The following dispatch has been received from Vice-Admiral Sir F. C. Doveton Sturdee, K.C.B., C.V.O., C.M.G., reporting the action off the Falkland Islands on Tuesday, the 8th of December, 1914:—

Invincible at Sea,
December 19th, 1914.

Sir,

I have the honour to forward a report on the action which took place on 8th December, 1914, against a German Squadron off the Falkland Islands.

I have the honour to be, Sir,
Your obedient Servant,
F. C. D. STURDEE,
Vice-Admiral, Commander-in-Chief.

The Secretary, Admiralty.

(A)—PRELIMINARY MOVEMENTS

The squadron, consisting of H.M. ships *Invincible*, flying my flag, Flag Captain Percy T. H. Beamish; *Inflexible*, Captain Richard F. Phillimore; *Carnarvon*, flying the flag of Rear-Admiral Archibald P. Stoddart, Flag Captain Harry L. d'E. Skipwith; *Cornwall*, Captain Walter M. Ellerton; Kent, Captain John D. Allen; *Glasgow*, Captain John Luce; *Bristol*, Captain Basil H. Fanshawe; and *Macedonia*, Captain Bertram S. Evans; arrived at Port Stanley, Falkland Islands, at 10.30

A.M. on Monday, the 7th December, 1914. Coaling was commenced at once, in order that the ships should be ready to resume the search for the enemy's squadron the next evening, the 8th December.

At 8 A.M. on Tuesday, the 8th December, a signal was received from the signal station on shore:

"A four-funnel and two-funnel man-of-war in sight from Sapper Hill, steering northwards."

At this time, the positions of the various ships of the squadron were as follows:

Macedonia — At anchor as look-out ship.
Kent (guard ship) — At anchor in Port William.
Invincible and *Inflexible* — In Port William.
Carnarvon — In Port William.
Cornwall — In Port William.
Glasgow — In Port Stanley.
Bristol — In Port Stanley.

The *Kent* was at once ordered to weigh, and a general signal was made to raise steam for full speed.

At 8.20 A.M. the signal station reported another column of smoke in sight to the southward, and at 8.45 A.M. the *Kent* passed down the harbour and took up a station at the entrance.

The *Canopus*, Captain Heathcoat S. Grant, reported at 8.47 A.M. that the first two ships were 8 miles off, and that the smoke reported at 8.20 A.M. appeared to be the smoke of two ships about 20 miles off.

At 8.50 A.M. the signal station reported a further column of smoke in sight to the southward.

The *Macedonia* was ordered to weigh anchor on the inner side of the other ships, and await orders.

At 9.20 A.M. the two leading ships of the enemy (*Gneisenau* and *Nürnberg*), with guns trained on the wireless station, came within range of the *Canopus*, who opened fire at them across the low land at a range of 11,000 yards. The enemy at once hoisted their colours and turned away. At this time the masts and smoke of the enemy were visible from the upper bridge of the *Invincible* at a range of approximately 17,000 yards across the low land to the south of Port William.

A few minutes later the two cruisers altered course to port, as though to close the *Kent* at the entrance to the harbour, but about this time it seems that the *Invincible* and *Inflexible* were seen over the land, as the enemy at once altered course and increased speed to join their consorts.

The *Glasgow* weighed and proceeded at 9.40 A.M. with orders to join the *Kent* and observe the enemy's movements.

At 9.45 A.M. the squadron—less the *Bristol*—weighed, and proceeded out of harbour in the following order: *Carnarvon, Inflexible, Invincible,* and *Cornwall*. On passing Cape Pembroke Light, the five ships of the enemy appeared clearly in sight to the south-east, hull down. The visibility was at its maximum, the sea was calm, with a bright sun, a clear sky, and a light breeze from the north-west.

At 10.20 A.M. the signal for a general chase was made. The battle-cruisers quickly passed ahead of the *Carnarvon* and overtook the *Kent*. The *Glasgow* was ordered to keep two miles from the *Invincible*, and the *Inflexible* was stationed on the starboard quarter of the flagship. Speed was eased to 20 knots at 11.15 A.M. to enable the other cruisers to get into station. At this time the enemy's funnels and bridges showed just above the horizon.

Information was received from the *Bristol* at 11.27 A.M. that three enemy ships had appeared off Port Pleasant, probably colliers or transports. The *Bristol* was therefore directed to take the *Macedonia* under his orders and destroy transports.

The enemy were still maintaining their distance, and I decided, at 12.20 P.M., to attack with the two battle-cruisers and the *Glasgow*.

At 12.47 P.M. the signal to "Open fire and engage the enemy" was made.

The *Inflexible* opened fire at 12.55 P.M. from her fore turret at the right-hand ship of the enemy, a light cruiser; a few minutes later the *Invincible* opened fire at the same ship.

The deliberate fire from a range of 16,500 to 15,000 yards at the right-hand light cruiser, who was dropping astern, became too threatening, and when a shell fell close alongside her at 1.20 P.M. she (the *Leipzig*) turned away, with the *Nürnberg* and *Dresden* to the south-west. These light cruisers were at once followed by the *Kent, Glasgow,* and *Cornwall,* in accordance with my instructions.

The action finally developed into three separate encounters, besides the subsidiary one dealing with the threatened landing.

(B) — ACTION WITH THE ARMOURED CRUISERS

The fire of the battle-cruisers was directed on the *Scharnhorst* and *Gneisenau*. The effect of this was quickly seen, when at 1.25 P.M., with the *Scharnhorst* leading, they turned about 7 points to port in succession into line-ahead and opened fire at 1.30 P.M. Shortly afterwards speed was eased to 24 knots, and the battle-cruisers were ordered to turn together, bringing them into line-ahead, with the *Invincible* leading.

The range was about 13,500 yards at the final turn, and increased until, at 2 P.M., it had reached 16,450 yards.

The enemy then (2.10 P.M.) turned away about 10 points to starboard and a second chase ensued, until, at 2.45 P.M., the battle-cruisers again opened fire; this caused the enemy, at 2.53 P.M., to turn into line-ahead to port and open fire at 2.55 P.M.

The *Scharnhorst* caught fire forward, but not seriously, and her fire slackened perceptibly; the *Gneisenau* was badly hit by the *Inflexible*.

At 3.30 P.M. the *Scharnhorst* led round about 10 points to starboard; just previously her fire had slackened perceptibly, and one shell had shot away her third funnel; some guns were not firing, and it would appear that the turn was dictated by a desire to bring her starboard guns into action. The effect of the fire on the *Scharnhorst* became more and more apparent in consequence of smoke from fires, and also escaping steam; at times a shell would cause a large hole to appear in her side, through which could be seen a dull red glow of flame. At 4.4 P.M. the *Scharnhorst*, whose flag remained flying to the last, suddenly listed heavily to port, and within a minute it became clear that she was a doomed ship; for the list increased very rapidly until she lay on her beam ends, and at 4.17 P.M. she disappeared.

The *Gneisenau* passed on the far side of her late flagship, and continued a determined but ineffectual effort to fight the two battle-cruisers.

At 5.8 P.M. the forward funnel was knocked over and remained resting against the second funnel. She was evidently in serious straits, and her fire slackened very much.

At 5.15 P.M. one of the *Gneisenau's* shells struck the *Invincible*; this was her last effective effort.

At 5.30 P.M. she turned towards the flagship with a heavy list to starboard, and appeared stopped, with steam pouring from her escape pipes and smoke from shell and fires rising everywhere. About this time I ordered the signal "Cease fire," but before it was hoisted the *Gneisenau* opened fire again, and continued to fire from time to time with a single gun.

At 5.40 P.M. the three ships closed in on the *Gneisenau*, and at this time the flag flying at her fore truck was apparently hauled down, but the flag at the peak continued flying.

At 5.50 P.M. "Cease fire" was made.

At 6 P.M. the *Gneisenau* heeled over very suddenly, showing the men gathered on her decks and then walking on her side as she lay for a minute on her beam ends before sinking.

The prisoners of war from the *Gneisenau* report that, by the time the ammunition was expended, some 600 men had been killed and wounded. The surviving officers and men were all ordered on deck and told to provide themselves with hammocks and any articles that could support them in the water.

When the ship capsized and sank there were probably some 200 unwounded survivors in the water, but, owing to the shock of the cold water, many were drowned within sight of the boats and ship.

Every effort was made to save life as quickly as possible both by boats and from the ships; life-buoys were thrown and ropes lowered, but only a proportion could be rescued. The *Invincible* alone rescued 108 men, 14 of whom were found to be dead after being brought on board; these men were buried at sea the following day with full military honours.

(C) — ACTION WITH THE LIGHT CRUISERS

At about 1 P.M., when the *Scharnhorst* and *Gneisenau* turned to port to engage the *Invincible* and *Inflexible*, the enemy's light cruisers turned to starboard to escape; the *Dresden* was leading and the *Nürnberg* and *Leipzig* followed on each quarter.

In accordance with my instructions, the *Glasgow*, *Kent*, and *Cornwall* at once went in chase of these ships; the *Carnarvon*, whose speed was insufficient to overtake them, closed the battle-cruisers.

The *Glasgow* drew well ahead of the *Cornwall* and *Kent*, and at 3 P.M. shots were exchanged with the *Leipzig* at 12,000 yards. The *Glasgow's* object was to endeavour to outrange the *Leipzig* with her 6-inch guns and thus cause her to alter coarse and give the *Cornwall* and *Kent* a chance of coming into action.

At 4.17 P.M. the *Cornwall* opened fire, also on the *Leipzig*.

At 7.17 P.M. the *Leipzig* was on fire fore and aft, and the *Cornwall* and *Glasgow* ceased fire.

The *Leipzig* turned over on her port side and disappeared at 9 P.M. Seven officer and eleven men were saved.

At 3.36 P.M. the *Cornwall* ordered the *Kent* to engage the *Nürnberg*, the nearest cruiser to her.

Owing to the excellent and strenuous efforts of the engine room department, the *Kent* was able to get within range of the *Nürnberg* at 5 P.M. At 6.35 P.M. the *Nürnberg* was on fire forward and ceased firing. The Kent also ceased firing and closed to 3,300 yards; as the colours were still observed to be flying in the *Nürnberg*, the *Kent* opened fire again. Fire was finally stopped five minutes later on the colours being hauled down, and every preparation was made to save life. The *Nürnberg* sank at 7.27 P.M., and as she sank a group of men were waving a German ensign attached to a staff. Twelve men were rescued, but only seven survived.

The *Kent* had four killed and twelve wounded, mostly caused by one shell.

During the time the three cruisers were engaged with the *Nürnberg* and *Leipzig*, the *Dresden*, who was beyond her consorts, effected her escape owing to her superior speed. The *Glasgow* was the only cruiser with sufficient speed to have had any chance of success. However, she was fully employed in engaging the *Leipzig* for over an hour before either the *Cornwall* or *Kent* could come up and get within range. During this time the *Dresden* was able to increase her distance and get out of sight.

The weather changed after 4 P.M., and the visibility was much reduced; further, the sky was overcast and cloudy, thus assisting the *Dresden* to get away unobserved.

(D)—ACTION WITH THE ENEMY'S TRANSPORTS

A report was received at 11.27 A.M. from H.M.S. *Bristol* that three ships of the enemy, probably transports or colliers, had appeared off Port Pleasant. The *Bristol* was ordered to take the *Macedonia* under his orders and destroy the transports.

H.M.S. *Macedonia* reports that only two ships, steamships *Baden* and *Santa Isabel*, were present; both ships were sunk after the removal of the crew.

I have pleasure in reporting that the officers and men under my orders carried out their duties with admirable efficiency and coolness, and great credit is due to the Engineer Officers of all the ships, several of which exceeded their normal full speed.

The names of the following are specially mentioned:

Officers

Commander Richard Herbert Denny Townsend, H.M.S. *Invincible*.

Commander Arthur Edward Frederick Bedford, H.M.S. *Kent*.

Lieutenant-Commander Wilfrid Arthur Thompson, H.M.S. *Glasgow*.

Lieutenant-Commander Hubert Edward Danreuther, First and Gunnery Lieutenant, H.M.S. *Invincible*.

Engineer-Commander George Edward Andrew, H.M.S. *Kent*.

Engineer-Commander Edward John Weeks, H.M.S. *Invincible*.

Paymaster Cyril Sheldon Johnson, H.M.S. *Invincible*.

Carpenter Thomas Andrew Walls, H.M.S. *Invincible*.

Carpenter William Henry Venning, H.M.S. *Kent*.

Carpenter George Henry Egford, H.M.S. *Cornwall*.

Petty Officers and Men

Ch. P.O. D. Leighton, O.N. 124238, *Kent*.

P.O., 2nd Cl., M. J. Walton (R.F.R., A1756), O.N. 118358, *Kent*.

Ldg. Smn. F. S. Martin, O.N. 233301, *Invincible*, Gnr's Mate, Gunlayer, 1st Cl.

Sigmn. F. Glover, O.N. 225731, *Cornwall*.

Ch. E. R. Art., 2nd Cl., J. G. Hill, O.N. 269646, *Cornwall*.

Actg. Ch. E. R. Art., 2nd Cl., R. Snowdon, O.N. 270654, *Inflexible*.

E. R. Art., 1st Cl., G. H. F. McCarten, O.N. 270023, *Invincible*.

Stkr. P.O. G. S. Brewer, O.N. 150950, *Kent*.

Stkr. P.O. W. A. Townsend, O.N. 301650, *Cornwall*.

Stkr., 1st Cl., J. Smith, O.N. SS 111915, *Cornwall*.

Shpwrt., 1st Cl., A. N. E. England, O.N. 341971, *Glasgow*.

Shpwrt., 2nd Cl., A. C. H. Dymott, O.N. M. 8047, *Kent*.

Portsmouth R.F.R.B.-3307 Sergeant Charles Mayes, H.M.S. *Kent*.

F. C. D. STURDEE.

BATTLE OF FALKLAND ISLANDS,

December 8th, 1914.

MESSAGES OF CONGRATULATION.

H.M.S. *Invincible*.
11th December, 1914.

Memorandum.

The following copy of a telegram received from the Admiralty, and the reply thereto, are forwarded for information. Both of these messages are to be read to the whole Ship's Company on the Quarter Deck of H.M. Ships under your command.

(Signed) F. C. D. Sturdee,
Vice-Admiral,
Commander-in-Chief.

The Rear-Admiral and Officers Commanding
H.M. Ships,
South Atlantic and South Pacific Squadron.

For Admiral, *Invincible*. (*Date*) 9.12.14

From Admiralty.

The following message has been received for you from His Majesty:—

I heartily congratulate you and your officers and men on your most opportune victory.

George R.I.

2. Our thanks are due to yourself and to officers and men for the brilliant victory you have reported.

Reply to His Majesty:

Your Majesty's gracious message has been received with pride and satisfaction by myself, the Rear-Admiral, Captains, Officers, and Ship's Companies under my command.

We hope soon to have the privilege of completing our mission by disposing of the remaining cruiser.

Commander-in-Chief, *Invincible*.

Reply to Their Lordships:

Admiralty congratulations not received till to-day. Myself, officers and men desire to thank their Lordships for the approbation of our efforts.

From C.-in-C. Home Fleets, H.M.S. *Cyclops*.

(*Date*) 10.12.14. 1.14 A.M.

With reference to your telegram 485[10] may I be permitted to offer my sincere congratulations on the splendid success attending your dispositions.

From Admiral, *Marseillaise, Brest*.

(*Date*) 10.12.14.

To Naval Attaché.

I beg to express to the Admiralty how fully I share their joy at the brilliant revenge taken by the British Navy at the Falklands.

F.N.A. Office.

From Petrograd.

To Vice-Admiral Sturdee, *Admiralty, London*.

(*Date*) 12.12.14. 3.0 A.M.

Please accept Heartiest Congratulations from the Russian Navy for the Brilliant Action of your Squadron in fighting the Enemy and sweeping out the oceans.

Vice-Admiral Roussie Nomer.

From C.-in-C. Home Fleets, H.M.S. *Cyclops*.

(*Date*) 11.12.14. 4.58 A.M.

Submit the hearty congratulation of the Grand Fleet on his victory may be conveyed to Admiral Sturdee.

Messages exchanged between H.E. the Governor of the Falkland Islands and C.-in-C. South Atlantic and Pacific:

Governor *to* Vice-Admiral:

11th December, 1914.

Warmest congratulations from self and Colony on your Victory.

Vice-Admiral *to* Governor:

May I thank you and the Colony for myself, the R.A., Captains, Officers and men of the Squadron for your congratulations on our success, which will not be complete until *Dresden* is accounted for. We wish to convey our thanks for the early warning of the approach of the enemy due to the good lookout from Sapper's Hill.

We feel the honour that the *Canopus* and the Squadron were in a position to prevent an old British Colony from being insulted or injured in any way, and hope that the enemy will have been taught a lesson not to repeat such action against any other part of the British Empire.

This Memorandum is to be read to whole Ship's Company on the Quarter Deck.

Invincible, at Port William,
11th December, 1914.

Memorandum.

The Commander-in-Chief wishes to congratulate all the ships of the squadron on the success of their main encounter with the enemy's squadron, and to thank the Rear-Admiral, Captains, Officers and Men for their individual assistance in attaining this great result. The zeal and steadiness under fire of all hands were most noticeable.

2. The victory will not be complete until the remaining cruiser is accounted for, and directly the squadron is coaled a further organised search will be made.

3. One of the greatest merits of the action is the small list of casualties due to the able handling of the ships by their Captains, who utilised the power of the guns and the speed of the ships to the best advantage. Further, the effective fire at long range and the thorough organization were very evident and enabled the action to be fought with success against a foe who displayed splendid courage, determination and efficiency.

4. The excellent way in which the Engine Room Departments responded to a sudden and unexpected demand reflects great credit on the officers and the whole engine room complements—this demand was made at a time when ships were coaling and making good defects during the few hours the ships were in harbour.

5. The successful disposal of the two powerful cruisers, two of the three light cruisers, and two colliers, will be of great advantage to the Naval Strategy of the British Empire.

6. Therefore all concerned can feel that they have performed a National Service on the 8th December, 1914, off the Falkland Islands.

(Signed) F. C. D. Sturdee,
Vice-Admiral,
Commander-in-Chief.

The Rear-Admiral, Captains, Officers, and all concerned, South Atlantic and South Pacific Squadron.

GALLANT SERVICES

"KENT" SERGEANT'S BRAVE DEED

Lord Chamberlain's Office,
St. James's Palace, S.W.,
3rd March, 1915.

The King has been graciously pleased to give orders for the following appointment to the Most Honourable Order of the Bath in recognition of the services of the undermentioned Officer mentioned in the foregoing dispatch:—

To be an Additional Member of the Military Division of the Third Class or Companion:

Captain John Luce, Royal Navy.

Admiralty, S.W.,
3rd March, 1915.

The King has been graciously pleased to give orders for the award of the *Distinguished Service Cross* to the undermentioned officers in recognition of their services mentioned in the foregoing dispatch:—

Carpenter Thomas Andrew Walls.
Carpenter William Henry Venning.
Carpenter George Henry Egford.

The following awards have also been made:—

To receive the Conspicuous Gallantry Medal:

Portsmouth R.F.R.B.-3307 Sergeant Charles Mayes, H.M.S. *Kent*. A shell burst and ignited some cordite charges in the casemate; a flash of flame went down the hoist into the ammunition passage. Sergeant Mayes picked up a charge of cordite and threw it away. He then got hold of a fire hose and flooded the compartment, extinguishing the fire in some empty shell bags which were burning. The extinction of this fire saved a disaster which might have led to the loss of the ship.

To receive the Distinguished Service Medal:

Chf. P.O. D. Leighton, O.N. 124238.
P.O., 2nd Cl., M. J. Walton (R.F.R., A1756), O.N. 118358.
Ldg. Smn. F. S. Martin, O.N. 233301, Gnr's Mate, Gunlayer, 1st Cl.

Sigmn. F. Glover, O.N. 225731.
Chf. E.-R. Artr., 2nd Cl., J. G. Hill, O.N. 269646.
Actg. Chf. E.-R. Artr., 2nd Cl., R. Snowdon, O.N. 270654.
E.-R. Artr., 1st Cl., G. H. F. McCarten, O.N. 270023.
Stkr. P.O. G. S. Brewer, O.N. 150950.
Stkr. P.O. W. A. Townsend, O.N. 301650.
Stkr., 1st Cl., J. Smith, O.N. SS 111915.
Shpwrt., 1st Cl., A. N. E. England, O.N. 341971.
Shpwrt., 2nd Cl., A. C. H. Dymott, O.N. M. 8047.

The following officers subsequently received recognition:—

Vice-Admiral Sir F. C. Doveton Sturdee, K.C.B., C.V.O., C.M.G., was honoured with a Baronetcy of the United Kingdom.

To be made Companions of the military division of the Bath:—

Captain John Luce (H.M.S. *Glasgow*).
Captain J. D. Allen (H.M.S. *Kent*).

Engineer-Commander E. J. Weeks was promoted to Acting Engineer-Captain.

The 1st Lieutenants of the *Invincible, Inflexible, Cornwall, Kent,* and *Glasgow* were all promoted to the rank of Commander in the next batch of promotions on December 31st, 1914:—

Lieutenant-Commander J. Wolfe-Murray (*Cornwall*).
Lieutenant-Commander H. E. Danreuther (*Invincible*).
Lieutenant-Commander W. A. Thompson (*Glasgow*).
Lieutenant-Commander E . L. Wharton (*Kent*).
Lieutenant-Commander R. H. C. Verner (*Inflexible*).

Engineer Lieutenant-Commander J. F. Shaw, the senior officer of his rank in the squadron, was promoted to Engineer Commander.

LIST OF BRITISH CASUALTIES

AT THE FALKLAND ISLANDS

The following is the complete revised casualty list of the action off the Falkland Islands on December 8th, 1914:—

H.M.S. "GLASGOW"

Killed.—Martell, E. H., stoker petty officer, Po./310682.

Dangerously wounded.—Bridger, M. J. E., A.B., Po./J7095.

Severely wounded. — Ford, H. B. S., signalman, Po./J4597; Major, P. E., shipwright 2nd class, Po./344489; Scotchmer, A. D., A.B., Po./232275.

H.M.S. "INFLEXIBLE"

Killed. — Livingstone, N., A.B., (R.F.R., Ch./B3593), Ch./190790.

Slightly wounded. — Hasler, T., ord. seaman, Ch./J18032; Mayes, A., seaman, R.N.R., 4754A; Spratt, G. F., A.B., Ch./237219.

H.M.S. "KENT"

Killed. — Kelly, S., pte., R.M.L.I. (R.F.R., A366), Po./3793; Kind, W. J., pte., R.M.L.I., Po./15049; Titheridge, A. C., pte., R.M.L.I. (R.F.R., B1254), Po./11220; Wood, W., pte. R.M.L.I., Po./16920; Young, W., seaman, R.N.R., 2543C.

Died of wounds. — Duckett, G. A., officers' steward 1st cl., Po./L2428; Snow, G., pte., R.M.L.I., Po./16858; Spence, T., sergt., R.M.L.I. (R.F.R., A811), Po./5674.

Wounded. — Arnold, W. P., R.M.L.I. (R.F.R., B860), Po./8302; Brewer, G. S., stoker petty officer (R.F.R., A3572), Po./150950; Day, F. T., pte., R.M.L.I. (R.F.R., A1008), Ch./6517; Lindsey, H., stoker 1st cl. (R.F.R., B3754), Po./SS101403; Joy, E., lance-corporal R.M.L.I. (R.F.R., B659), Po./10568; Pear, J., stoker 1st cl. (R.F.R., 4172), Po./SS102840; Restall, J., stoker 1st cl. (R.F.R., B4055), Po./291073; Sheridan, A. P., pte., R.M.L.I., Po./13708.

THE "DRESDEN": ACTION WITH "KENT" AND "GLASGOW"

The Secretary of the Admiralty makes the following announcement:—

On 14th March, at 9 A.M., H.M.S. *Glasgow*, Captain John Luce, C.B., R.N.; H.M. Auxiliary Cruiser *Orama*, Captain John R. Segrave, R.N.; and H.M.S. *Kent*, Captain John D. Allen, C.B., R.N., caught the *Dresden* near Juan Fernandez Island.

An action ensued. After five minutes' fighting the *Dresden* hauled down her colours and displayed the white flag.

She was much damaged and set on fire, and after she had been burning for some time her magazine exploded, and she sank.

The crew were saved. Fifteen badly wounded Germans are being landed at Valparaiso.

There were no British casualties, and no damage to the ships.

Appendix

A LIST OF OFFICERS SERVING
IN THE ACTIONS RECORDED IN
THE NARRATIVE

A List of Officers serving in the Ships that took part in the Actions recorded in the Narrative.

H.M.S. "CARMANIA"
Armed Merchantman

Captain	Noel Grant
Com. R.N.R.	James Barr
Lieutenant	Edmund L. B. Lockyer
Lieut.-Com. R.N.R.	Wm. J. O'Neill
Lieut. R.N.R.	Peter A. Murchie
	E. B. Dalby
	Walter C. Battle
	J. Henessey
	M. F. Murray
	William V. Ogley *(act.)*
	A. Parnis *(act.)*
Ch. Eng. R.N.R.	Francis Drummond
Sen. Eng. R.N.R.	James Mcdonald
Eng. R.N.R.	Robert Craig
	Alexander Lindsay
	Claude Shore
	Robert Wilson
	John O. Teare

	James Duncan
	Harold Kendall
	Charles Rennie
	Walt Fraser
	James McPherson
Fleet-Surgeon	A. Cropley *(ret.)*
Tempy. Surgeon	E. Maynard
	Harry Clough
Ch. Gunner	Henry Middleton
Act. Sub-Lieutenant	G. F. Dickens
Asst. Eng. R.N.R.	Joseph Verdin
	Albert E. Brittlebank
	Percival J. Thompson
Asst. Paym. R.N.R. (in charge)	Walter H. Ramsden
Asst. Paym. R.N.R.	Arthur H. Burden
	Ernest W. Turney
Midshipman R.N.R.	William Man
	D. N. Colson
	E. R. Linger-Burton *(proby.)*
	J. R. Bane *(proby.)*
	W. Barr *(proby.)*
	R. P. Nisbet *(proby.)*
	J. B. Mein *(proby.)*

H.M.S. "GOOD HOPE"

Armoured Cruiser

Rear-Admiral	Sir Christopher G. F. M. Cradock, K.C.V.O., C.B.
Personal Staff	

Secretary	George B. Owens
Flag Lieut.-Com.	George E. Cumming
Lieut. R.M.	Harold S. Walker
Clerk to Sec.	John Egremont
	Edward C. Webber
Captain	Philip Francklin, M.V.O.
Commander	Arthur T. Darley
	Walter Scott
Lieut.-Commander	Percival Van Straubenzee
	Gerald B. Gaskell
	Godfrey B. J. Benyon
Lieutenant	Lancelot A. Montgomery
	Gordon E. E. Gray
	John M. H. Fisher
	Douglas C. Tudor
	Arthur G. Smith
Lieutenant R.N.R.	Edward J. French
Eng. Com.	Arthur Brown
Eng. Lieut.-Com.	Herbert W. Couch
Major R.M.	Frederick C. Edwards
Chaplain	Rev. Arthur H. J. Pitt
Fleet Surgeon	James J. Walsh, M.B.
Fleet Paym.	Alfred H. Veitch
Surgeon	Francis C. Searle
Surgeon (Reserve)	Ferdinand L. J. M. de Verteuil, M.B.
Sub-Lieutenant (act.)	Francis J. A. Cotter
Asst. Paym.	John E. Tizard
	Stuart Watson

Ch. Gunner	George F. Organ
Ch. Sig. Boatswain	William Penny
Boatswain	Franklyn F. Stephens
	John W. Bushell
Warrant Officer (act.)	Robert C. T. Roe
Gunner	William D. Wright
	Francis A. G. Oakley
	Robert J. Page *(act.)*
	William W. Kingdom *(act.)*
Carpenter	Albert J. Hellyer
Artif. Eng.	Richard M. Healy
	William R. Henon
	Joseph Duckworth
Wt. Mechanician	William A. Bass
Mid. R.C.N.	W. A. Palmer
	F. V. W. Hathaway
	A. W. Silver
	M. Cann
Mid. R.N.R.	Graham Trounson *(proby.)*
	Henry K. D. Cuthbert *(proby.)*
	Geoffrey M. Dowding *(proby.)*
Asst. Clerk	Charles G. Cook *(tempy.)*
Naval Cadet	G. Coffin
	I. M. R. Campbell
	S. M. Raw
	D. A. Willey
	R. A. Macdonald

H.M.S. "MONMOUTH"
Armoured Cruiser

Captain	Frank Brandt
Commander	Spencer D. Forbes
Lieut.-Commander	Bertie W. Bluett
	Hugh D. Collins
	Hon. Peter R. H. D. Willoughby
Lieutenant	John A. Lees
	Thomas Stapleton
	Harry P. Rogers
	Alfred Edgar
	Wilfred D. Stirling
	Maurice J. H. Bagot
Eng. Com.	John B. Wilshin
Eng. Lieutenant	Bernard C. Child
	Lionel B. Wansbrough
Captain R.M.	Geoffrey M. I. Herford
Chaplain	— — —
Staff Surgeon	Henry Woods
Fleet Paym.	John Cooper
Surgeon	Albert J. Tonkinson
Sub-Lieutenant	Hanway Cooper
Asst. Paym.	Douglas B. Lee
Ch. Gunner	Robert T. H. V. Lee
Ch. Carpenter	Frederick G. Hartland
Gunner	James Bennett
Boatswain	William J. Barrett
	Thomas B. Ireland (act.)

Artif. Eng.	George H. Farebrother
	Alfred T. Johns
	William Day
Wt. Mechanician	Alfred Start
Wt. Eng. R.N.R.	Charles Driver
Clerk	Basil St. M. Cardew
Asst. Clerk	Cecil T. Martin *(tempy.)*
Naval Cadet	K. A. M. Somerville
	G. R. Bruce
	J. F. Boulton
	V. G. E. S. Schreiber
	J. R. Le G. Pullen
	F. A. Cooper
	C. Musgrave
	J. M. Pascoe
	G. W. Muir
	P. S. Candy

H.M.S. "GLASGOW"
Light Cruiser

Captain	John Luce
Lieut.-Commander	Wilfred A. Thompson
	Charles L. Backhouse
	Maurice P. B. Portman
Lieutenant	Herbert I. N. Lyon
	Charles G. Stuart
Lieut. R.N.R.	Walter M. Knowles
	T. W. F. Winter

Sub-Lieutenant	Frederick B. Alison
Eng. Lieut.-Com.	Percy J. Shrubsole
Eng. Lieut.	John S. Machan
Fleet Surgeon	Robert T. Gilmour
Staff Surgeon	Alexander T. Wysard *(ret.)*
Staff Paymaster	Francis E. Adams
Asst. Paym.	Lloyd Hirst
	Norman H. Beall
Gunner	Arthur G. Foreman
	William R. Heilbroun
	George H. Bartlett
Carpenter	Sylvester G. Pawley
Artif. Eng.	Charles A. Palser
	James Milne *(act.)*
Midshipman R.N.R.	George W. Wilson

H.M.S. "OTRANTO"
Armed Merchantman

Captain	Herbert M. Edwards
Commander R.N.R.	Walter de M. Baynham, R.D.
Lieutenant	Julian M. Ogilvie
Lieutenant R.N.R.	T. B. Storey
	H. W. Woodcock
	H. G. Thompson
	R. M. Ward
	F. R. O'Sullivan
	A. W. Clemson
Ch. Eng. R.N.R.	David Montgomery
Sen. Eng. R.N.R.	William J. Philip

Engineer R.N.R.	William Mackersie
	Robert Pittendrigh
	Andrew Allen
	Adam A. I. Kirk
Tempy. Surgeon	W. Meikle
	S. Robertson
Sub-Lieutenant R.N.R.	G. F. Willdigg
	R. Roscoe
Asst. Eng. R.N.R.	Alan Cameron
	Peter Brown
	Thomas R. Blellock
	Alexander C. Mearns
	John Gemmell
	Aymer. R. McDougall
	William McL. Allan
Asst. Paym. R.N.R.	Roland H. Draper
	Thomas B. Wildman
Gunner	W. J. Drew *(ret.)*
Midshipman R.N.R.	Charles E. F. St. John
	Herbert J. Anchor
	George D. Scott
	George E. D. Billam
	D. N. White
	C. C. Lawrence

H.M.S. "CANOPUS"

Captain	Heathcote S. Grant
Commander	Philip J. Stopford
Lieut.-Commander	Andrew Kerr *(ret.)*

	Philip Hordern
Lieutenant	Harry T. Bennett
	Henry N. Lesley
	Owen W. Phillips
Lieut.-Com. R.N.R.	Arthur H. Bird
Lieutenant R.N.R.	Charles T. Keigwin. R.D.
	Clarence Milner
	David M. Clarke *(act.)*
	William A. Williamson *(act.)*
	Malcolm C. Powell
Eng. Commander	William Denbow
Eng. Lieut.-Com.	Sydney P. Start
Captain R.M.L.I.	Gerald S. Hobson
Fleet Paymaster	Albert Greenwood
Lieutenant R.N.R.	Charles C. Cartwright
	William J. Donohue
Staff Surgeon	August J. Wernet
Tempy. Surgeon	Michael Vlaste
Surgeon R.N.V.R.	Charles H. F. Atkinson
Asst. Paym. R.N.R.	Harold E. W. Lutt
Chaplain	Rev. James D. de Vitre
Ch. Boatswain	John Myers
Gunner	James Irish
Boatswain	William Evans
	William E. T. Honey *(act.)*
Ch. Artificer Eng.	Walter G. Morris
Art. Eng.	Ernest E. Moorey
Wt. Eng. R.N.R.	T. W. Greenwood
Ch. Carpenter	Albert Hughes
Midshipman	C. R. O. Burge

	R. T. Young
	P. R. Malet de Carteret
	J. L. Storey
	H. M. L. Durrant
	R. H. L. Orde
	R. K. Dickson
	B. R. Cochrane
	L. H. P. Henderson
	L. H. V. Booth
Mate	R. C. T. Roe *(act.)*, left by Good Hope on an island at Vallenar Roads, Chile
Clerk	Jean le Jeune
Midshipman, R.N.R.	Lawrence H. Faragher

H.M.S. "CARNARVON"
Armoured Cruiser

Rear-Admiral	Archibald P. Stoddart
Secretary	Thomas R. Waterhouse
Flag Lieutenant	Hon. Humphrey A. Pakington
Clerk to Sec.	H. Guy Pertwee
Captain	Harry L. d'E. Skipwith
Commander	Thomas A. Williams
	Ronald E. Chilcott
Lieut.-Commander	Arthur S. Burt
	Arthur G. Leslie
	Ralph Leatham
Lieutenant	A. M. Donovan
	David B. Nicol
Lieutenant R.N.R.	Bertram Shillitoe

	Bertram H. Davies
Eng. Commander	Alfred T. P. Read
Eng. Lieutenant	Edward Iliff
Maj. R.M.	Edmund Wray
Captain R.M.	Arthur J. Mellor
Chaplain	Rev. John Beatty
Fleet Surgeon	Edward Cooper
Fleet Paym.	Albert E. B. Hosken
Surgeon	Arthur G. Valpy French
Surgeon R.N.V.R.	William H. Condell
Sub-Lieutenant	Philip F. Glover
	Frederick W. F. Cuddeford
Asst. Paym.	Herebert E. Symons
Gunner	William H. Hunt
	Sidney C. Woodriffe
	John F. Hannaford
	W. H. Ellis
Boatswain	Alfred Hill
	Albert E. Pearson
Sig. Boatswain	Herbert H. Hunwicks
Carpenter	Norman O. Staddon
Artif. Eng.	Harold E. Oyler
	Claude B. King
	James Telford
	Charles Hill
	William S. Branson
Clerk	Charles H. Doubleday
Midshipman	J. R. Warburton
	P. M. S. Blackett
	P. J. M. Penney

                    S. P. Broughton
                    A. C. Jelf
                    R. M. Dick
                    R. G. Fowle
                    C. J. M. Hamilton
                    J. C. E. A. Johnson
                    M. S. Graham
                    R. Mandley
                    L. H. Peppe

                H.M.S. "CORNWALL"
                Armoured Cruiser

Captain	Walter M. Ellerton
Commander	Herbert A. Buchanan-Wollaston
Lieut.-Commander	James Wolfe-Murray
	Henry E. H. Spencer-Cooper, M.V.O.
Lieutenant	Mansel B. F. Colvile
	Edward W. Sinclair
	Kenneth B. Millar
	Norman Whitehead
	John S. Hammill
	Robin E. Jeffreys
Sub-Lieutenant R.N.R.	Desmond A. Stride
	William H. Richardson
Eng. Commander	Archibald W. Maconochie
Eng. Lieutenant	Douglas G. Campbell
	Cecil J. Meggs
Captain R.M.	Herbert R. Brewer
Chaplain and N.I.	Robert McKew, B.A., B.D.
Fleet Surgeon	Malcolm Cameron

Fleet Paymaster	Harry G. Wilson
Naval Inst.	Chas. S. P. Franklin, B.A.
	George H. Andrew, M.A.
Surgeon	Cecil R. M. Baker
Asst. Paym.	Henry Rogers
Asst. Paym. R.N.R.	Joseph H. Wilson
Ch. Art. Eng.	Thomas R. I. Crabb
	Edwin C. Edwards
Gunner	Ernest Stone
	Richard F. Hall
	Edward W. Pearne (T.)
Boatswain	Ernest H. Gearing
Carpenter	George H. Egford
Art. Eng.	Percy S. Walkey
	Edwin Foster
Midshipman	Philip F. Armstrong
	Arthur H. Ashworth
	Hugh E. Burnaby
	John Bostock
	Douglas M. Branson
	Lycett Gardiner
	Jocelyn S. Bethell
	Morice Blood
	Richard F. Carter
	Willoughby N. Barstow
	Nigel D. Bury
	William S. Batson

H.M.S. "BRISTOL"
Light Cruiser

Captain	Basil H. Fanshawe

Commander	Harry L. Boyle
Lieut.-Commander	Ernest G. H. Du Boulay
Lieutenant	Robert F. U. P. Fitzgerald
	Archibald B. Cornabé
	Edward G. G. Hastings
Lieutenant R.N.R.	James A. Hodges
Eng. Commander	James D. W. H. F. Cranley
Eng. Lieutenant	Edward G. Sanders
Staff Surgeon	Leslie M. Morris
Staff Paym.	Tom Henley
Sub-Lieutenant	Cyril A. H. Brooking
	Charles H. L. Woodhouse
Gunner	Stephen W. Duckett
	George W. Callaway
Boatswain	Frank Box
Carpenter	William L. Harfield
Artif. Eng.	William Tearle
	Joseph L. Wagstaff
Clerk	John G. B. Collier
	James Hogg

H.M.S. "MACEDONIA"
Armed Merchantman

Captain	Bertram S. Evans, M.V.O.
Commander R.N.R.	Edwin P. Martin
Lieut.-Commander	Valentine D. English
Lieut.-Com. R.N.R.	Henry G. Westmore, R.D.
	W. F. Pollard
Lieutenant R.N.R.	W. C. Young
	T. C. W. Thompson

	F. Cross
Ch. Eng. R.N.R.	James G. Crichton
Sen. Eng. R.N.R.	Thomas S. Ferguson
Eng. R.N.R.	William C. O. Taylor
	Walter J. Hickingbotham
	James Finnecy
	George R. R. Cushing
	Edmund J. Caws
	Frederick P. Voisey
Tempy. Surgeon	A. M. Russell
Sub-Lieutenant R.N.R.	Alfred W. Drew
	E. F. Hannan
	O. Taylor
	Jeffery Elliott
Surg. Prob. R.N.V.R.	Harold Williamson
Asst. Eng. R.N.R.	Oliver J. R. Pinkney
	F. C. Masters
	Joseph Neale
	William G. Cheeseman
Asst. Paym. in charge	Herbert W. Landon
Asst. Paym. R.N.R.	Percy Selwin
Gunner	James W. Drew
Midshipman R.N.R.	H. J. Miller
	G. V. Thomas
	F. H. E. Firmstone
	Gordon D. Brown
	B. V. Rutley
	W. G. Hiscock

H.M.S. "ORAMA"
Armed Merchantman

Captain	John R. Segrave
Commander R.N.R.	John F. Healey, R.D.
Lieut.-Commander	Joseph W. L. Hunt
Lieut. R.N.R.	Geoffrey G. Thorne
	Edward S. Carver
	Henry T. Heale (ret.)
	Allen Fielding
	Frederick W. Willsden (ret.)
	T. P. Webb
	W. A. Assenheimer
Ch. Engineer	John Robertson
Sen. Engineer	Donald McL. McWilliam
Engineer	J. R. Dowling
	James Imrie
	H. P. Jack
	Alexander S. Hall
Asst. Engineer	Alexander Manson
	Neil H. T. Hill
	Charles W. Howil
	Donald Matheson
	David A. Sheeby
	David M. Johnston
	William Turner
	William Houston
	James Piggott
	James McAdam
	George Herd
Tempy. Surgeon	Herbert E. Scowcroft

Sub-Lieut. R.N.R.	Sydney Welham
	M. W. Cooksey
Asst. Paym. R.N.R.	Herbert Newman
	John F. Cooper
Ch. Gunner	Arthur J. Burstow
Midshipman R.N.R.	Edward Roberts
	Stuart F. Pocock
	Leonard E. Fordham
	Bernard K. Berry
	S. S. Adley
	H. Schofield
	H. C. C. Forsyth
	G. E. G. Sandercock

H.M.S. "INVINCIBLE"
Battle-Cruiser

Vice-Admiral	Sir F. C. Doveton Sturdee, K.C.B., C.V.O., C.M.G.
Secretary	Cyril S. Johnson
Flag Lieutenant	Reginald W. Blake
Clerk to Sec.	Arthur D. Duckworth
Captain	Percy T. H. Beamish
Commander	Richard H. D. Townsend
Lieut.-Commander	Hubert E. Dannreuther
	Hon. Edward B. S. Bingham
	John C. F. Borrett
	Lionel H. Shore
	Edward Smyth-Osbourne
Lieutenant	Cecil S. Sandford
	Cameron St. C. Ingham
	Hugh H. G. Begbie

Lieutenant R.N.R.	George ff. H. Lloyd
Eng. Commander	Edward J. Weeks
Eng. Lieut.-Commander	James F. Shaw
Eng. Lieutenant	Francis L. Mogg
Major R.M.	Robert C. Colquhoun
Captain R.M.	Charles H. Malden
Temp. Lieut. R.M.	John T. Le Seelleur
Chaplain	Rev. Arthur C. Moreton, M.A.
Fleet Paym.	Ernest W. Mainprice
Fleet Surgeon	Walter J. Bearblock
Surgeon	Ernest MacEwan
	Clarence E. Greeson, M.B.
Sub-Lieutenant	Alexander P. McMullen
	Robert R. Stewart
Asst. Paym.	Gordon Franklin
Asst. Paym. R.N.R.	Clement A. Woodland
Gunner	William C. Hunt
	Robert Connolly
	Mark W. Cameron
	Ernest J. Read
	Sydney C. Kennell
Boatswain	Frederick Luker
	Philip J. Warrington
	Wilfred Turner
Sig. Boatswain	William F. Raper
Gunner R.M.	Albert E. Nixon
Carpenter	Thomas A. Walls
Artf. Engineer	Walter H. Bull
	John Dews
	Frederick C. Fry
Clerk	William R. C. Steele
Midshipman	Gordon T. Campbell
	Edwin T. Hodgson
	Douglas A. C. Birch

John M. Shorland
John H. G. Esmonde
Allan G. McEwan
Rupert C. Montagu
Lionel D. Morse
Duncan G. Reid

H.M.S. "INFLEXIBLE"
Battle-Cruiser

Captain	Richard F. Phillimore, C.B., M.V.O.
Commander	Ernest Wigram
	John W. Carrington
Lieut.-Commander	Rudolf H. C. Verner
	Hon. Patrick G. E. C. Acheson, M.V.O.
	Frederic Giffard
	Ralph B. Janvrin
Lieutenant	Edward C. Denison
	Kenneth H. D. Acland
	Arthur W. Blaker
	Brian L. G. Sebastian
Lieutenant R.N.R.	Herbert J. Giles
Eng. Commander	Harry Lashmore
Eng. Lieut.-Commander	Arthur E. Lester
Eng. Lieutenant	Rey G. Parry
Major R.M.	John B. Finlaison
Captain R.M.	Robert Sinclair
Chaplain	Rev. Ernest S. Phillips, M.A.
Fleet Surgeon	Edward H. Meaden
Fleet Paym.	Henry Horniman
Surgeon	John H. B. Martin, M.B., B.A.
	Martyn H. Langford
Sub-Lieutenant (act.)	Thos. H. Welsby
	Alexander C. G. Madden

	Leicester St. J. Curzon-Howe
	Robert D. Oliver
	Alfred E. B. Giles
	John H. Macnair
	George T. Philip
	Terence H. Back
Asst. Paym.	John F. Stephens
Ch. Gunner	Edward Fox
Ch. Boatswain	Alfred M. Cady
Ch. Artf. Eng.	George E. Martin
Gunner	John H. Moore
	Frederick W. Furmadge
Boatswain	John A. Brander
Sig. Boatswain	Phillip J. Jones
Gunner R.M.	John Cameron
Carpenter	William A. Cawsey
Artf. Engineer	Charles A. Richards
Artf. Eng. (act.)	William S. Barnes
Bandmaster R.M.	Herbert Reely
Midshipman	Rupert E. Bethune
	John D. Chapple
	Regd. G. France-Hayhurst
	David D. Mercer
Clerk	Crichton F. Laborde

H.M.S. "KENT"
Armoured Cruiser

Captain	John D. Allen
Commander	Arthur E. F. Bedford
Lieut.-Commander	Eric L. Wharton
	James R. Harvey
Lieutenant	Victor H. Danckwerts
Lieut.-Com. R.N.R.	Charles M. Redhead, R.D.
Lieutenant R.N.R.	Harold T. Dunn

	Frederic C. Howard
	William G. B. Jones
	Walter R. Tilling
	James Marshall
	John L. S. G. Lilley
Eng. Commander	George E. Andrew
Eng. Lieutenant	Victor O. Foreman *(ret.)*
Captain R.M.	Robert W. J. Laing
Chaplain	Rev. Norman B. Kent, B.A.
Fleet Surgeon	Edward B. Pickthorn *(ret.)*
Paymaster	Sydney G. Andrews
Temp. Surg.	Ronald E. B. Burn
Surgeon R.N.V.R.	Thomas B. Dixon
Asst. Paym. R.N.R.	William G. Stewart
Gunner	Thomas P. Collins
	Claude H. Griffiths
Boatswain	William T. Dunning
	Walter H. Speed
Sig. Boatswain	Leonard C. Croucher
Carpenter	William H. Venning
Artf. Engineer	William Muirhead
Wt. Engineer R.N.R	John Garrow
	John W. Scott
	Donald Campbell
Midshipman R.N.R.	Robert L. Burridge
	John D. Ross
	David T. M. Williams
	George C. B. Liley
	Cecil B. Hogan
	Harold W. S. Wright
Midshipman R.N.R.	Frederick E. Valentine
	George W. Barker
	Edgar H. Cowan
Clerk	Reginald H. Kitchin

INDEX

Allardyce, the Hon. William, Governor of Falkland Islands

Allen, Captain J. D., of *Kent*
a tribute to crew of *Kent* by
created a C.B.

America (South), apprehension in
Germans in
scenery of

Asama in eastern Pacific

Atlantic (South), battle in

Australia joins North Pacific squadron

Baden sunk by *Bristol*

Barr, Acting-Commander James C., awarded C.B.

Battle-cruiser action, a

Beamish, Captain P. H., of *Invincible*

Boarding parties and their work

Brandt, Captain Frank, of *Monmouth*

Brazilian ports, enemy shipping at

Brewer, Stkr. P.O. G. S., a D.S.M. for

Bristol, officers of

opens fire on *Karlsruhe*

British casualties in the Falklands
men-of-war off South America

Canada purchases submarines

Canopus, an amusing incident on
converted into a floating fort
fine work of
good shooting by
officers of
skilful navigation of

Cap Trafalgar, sinking of
official dispatch on action

Carmania, a conflagration on
decorations for officers and men
heroism of crew
officers of
sinks *Cap Trafalgar et seq.*

Carnarvon, a German's toast
a valuable capture by
chases the enemy
officers of

Chilean coast, action off the (*see* Coronel, battle of)

China, German squadron in

Coaling, the "delights" of

Colson, Midshipman D.N., awarded D.S.C.

Concentration, necessity of

Cornwall chases enemy
decorations for crew
escorts *Carmania* to base

officers of
opens fire on *Leipzig*

Coronel, battle of *et seq.*
enemy torpedo attack at
official dispatches on
outstanding features of
unreliable accounts of
vessels engaged in
visibility conditions advantageous to enemy
von Spee's report on

Cradock, Rear-Admiral Sir Christopher, a tribute to
goes down with his ship
his command reinforced
his objective at Coronel
hoists his flag
sights and chases *Karlsruhe*

Crown of Galicia, German prisoners on

Danreuther, Lieut.-Com. H. E., promotion for

Defence essays to join southern command
sails for Cape Town

Dickens, Acting Sub-Lieut. G. F., awarded D.S.C.

Dresden, a vain search for
arrives at Orange Bay
chase of
eludes her pursuers
hoists the white flag, and sinks
joins von Spee
sinking of: Admiralty announcement on

Dymott, Shpwrt. A. C. H., awarded D.S.M.

Easter Island, German squadron at

Edinburgh Castle, deck hockey on

Edwards, Captain H. McI., of *Otranto*

Edwards, Mr., of Easter Island

Egford, Carpenter G. H., receives D.S.C.

Ellerton, Captain W. M., of *Cornwall*
efficient handling of his ship

Emden, exploits and sinking of

England, Shpwrt. A. N. E., a D.S.M. for

Evans, Captain B. S., of *Macedonia*

Falkland Islands, battle of, Admiral Sturdee's dispatch on
battle-cruiser action *et seq.*
British casualties in
commercial importance of
congratulations on
decisive nature of
enemy sighted
light cruiser action
the prize bounty
contemplated seizure of
land and sea defences of
topography of
why chosen as base

Fanning Island, British cable station destroyed at

Fanshawe, Captain B. H., of *Bristol*

Felton, Mrs., her services recognised

Food problem in wartime

Francklin, Captain Philip, of *Good Hope*

French colonies, Germans and

German barbarity, a typical instance of
casualties in the Falklands
4.1-inch gun, range of
light cruisers, chase of
men-of-war in foreign seas *et seq.*
sailors buried at sea

Germans abandon colonies in Polynesia
in South America

Germany, her responsibility for the war

Glasgow, a duel with *Leipzig*
casualties in Coronel battle
chases enemy cruisers
officers of
sights enemy

Glover, Signalman Frank, awarded D.S.M.

Gneisenau, a gallant fight by
accurate shooting by
end of
her commander rescued

Good Hope becomes Admiral Cradock's flagship
loss of
officers of

Grant, Captain Heathcoat, of *Canopus*

Grant, Captain Noel, of *Carmania*
awarded C.B.

Great Britain and German colonies
enters the War

Hague Conference and the law of neutrality

High explosives, curious examples of damage by

Hill, Chief Engine Room Artificer, awarded D.S.M.

Hizen in the Pacific

Idzuma in the Pacific

Inflexible, a fine run by
first shot in Falkland Islands battle
officers of

Invincible and Falkland Islands battle
damaged
joins Admiral Stoddart's squadron
lost in Jutland battle
officers of

Japan declares war

Japanese cruisers in the eastern Pacific

Karlsruhe, chase and escape of
end of

Kent, anxiety regarding fate of
casualties on
chases German cruisers
duel with *Nürnberg*
ensign of
officers of
opens fire on *Leipzig*
sights *Dresden*

Königsberg blocked up and destroyed

Kronprinz Wilhelm, escape of
internment of

Leatham, Captain E. La T., of *Defence*

Leighton, Chf. P.O. D., a D.S.M. for

Leipzig, a running fight by
chase of
eludes her pursuers
end of *et seq.*
joins von Spee's squadron
on fire
stories of survivors

Life at sea in 1914 *et seq.*

Lockyer, Lieut.-Commander E. L. B., awarded D.S.O.

Luce, Captain John, of *Glasgow*
and Falkland Islands battle
awarded C.B.
report on Coronel action

Lyddite shell in warfare

Macedonia conveys German prisoners
officers of

Magellan, Straits of

Maltzhan, Baron von

Martin, Ldg. Smn. F. S., awarded D.S.M.

Mas-a-Fuera, temporary headquarters of German squadron

Mayes, Sergt. Charles, brave deed recognised

McCarten, E.-R. Artr. G. H. F., awarded D.S.M.

Mera, voluntary internment of

Merchant ships, increased enemy sinkings of

Mersey destroys *Königsberg*

Middleton, Chief Gunner Henry, awarded D.S.C.

Monmouth in Coronel action
loss of
officers of

Murray, Lieut.-Com. J. Wolfe, promotion for

Napier, Captain W. R., of *Edinburgh Castle*

Naval actions, tactics of modern

Navarro sunk by *Orama*

Navy, the, life at sea *et seq.*
postal arrangements of
work in wartime

Newbolt, Sir Henry, on Admiral Cradock
on Falkland Islands battle

Newcastle in the North Pacific

Nürnberg, chase of
duel with *Kent*
joins von Spee's squadron
sinking of
sinks *Monmouth*

Orama, officers of
sinks a German storeship

Otranto, officers of

under enemy fire

Pacific (Western), the, German squadron in

Papeete, bombardment of
French gunboat sunk at

Patagonia, internment of

Pegasus, sinking of

Phillimore, Captain R. F., of *Inflexible*

Port Stanley, arrival of *Canopus*: the scene
description of

Port William, British squadron in

Postal arrangements at sea

Princess Royal in North American waters

Prinz Eitel Friedrich, internment of

Professor Woermann, capture of

Royal Naval Reserve, efficiency of

Sailors, the psychology of *et seq.*

Santa Isabel, sunk by *Bristol*

Scharnhorst badly hit
good marksmanship of
sinking of

Segrave, Captain J. R., of *Orana*

Serajevo tragedy, the

Severn and the end of *Königsberg*

Seydlitz, escape of

Shark fishing as a pastime

Shaw, Eng. Lieut.-Com. J. F., promotion for

Skipwith, Captain H. L. d'E., of *Carnarvon*

Smith, Stoker John, a D.S.M. for

Snowdon, Act.-Chf. E.-R. Artr. R., a D.S.M. for

South America (*see* America, South)

Spee, Vice-Admiral Count von, and his command
aims and hopes of *et seq.*
contemplates seizure of Falklands
death of
movements of his squadron
policy of, considered and analysed
refuses to drink a toast
report on Coronel battle

Stoddart, Rear-Admiral and a rescued kinsman
commands British squadron
reinforcements from England for
succeeds Admiral Cradock
transfers his flag

Sturdee, Vice-Admiral F. C. Doveton
a Baronetcy for
dispatch on battle of Falkland Islands *et seq.*
his strategic victory
in command of British squadron
ordered to Gibraltar

Submarines purchased by Canadian Government

Suffolk chases *Karlsruhe*

Sydney in action with *Emden*

Thompson, Lieut.-Com. W. A., promotion for

Titania, enemy auxiliary cruiser

Townsend, Stoker P.O. W. A., awarded D.S.M.

Tsingtau, German base at

Turner, Maj., commands Falkland Island Volunteers

Venning, Carpenter W. H., awarded D.S.C.

Verner, Lieut.-Com. R. H. C., promotion for

Walls, Carpenter T. A., awarded D.S.C.

Walton, P.O. M. J., a D.S.M. for

Weeks, Engineer-Com. E. J., promotion for

Wharton, Com., and sinking of *Nürnberg* promotion for

Wireless stations, German

FOOTNOTES:

[1] *Note.*—This book was completed in May, 1917, but was withheld from publication on account of the many omissions prescribed by the Naval Censor.

[2] The German Chancellor had publicly declared the intention to capture the French colonies.

[3] *See* Map

[4] *Carmania*, Cunard S.S. Co.—19,524 tons, 650 feet long, triple screw turbines.

Cap Trafalgar, Hamburg-Sud-Amerik S.S. Co.—18,710 tons, 590 feet long, triple screw turbines.

[5] According to "Brassey's Naval Annual."

[6] German wireless system.

[7] "Tales of the Great War" (Longmans).

[8] "Blackwood's Magazine."

[9] The *Seydlitz*—the German auxiliary that escaped—took in the wireless signal announcing the victory and actually heard the firing of the *Cornwall* and the *Glasgow* on her beam about four miles off. She managed to escape under cover of the fog by steering to the south, but it was a near thing.

[10] Reporting sinking of three German ships.